ROBERT DEGROOT

Leave a Legacy of Legendary Customer Service

An Attitude and Skills-Based Approach

For inquiries:

ROBERT DEGROOT

Bob@SalesHelp.com

HTTPS://SalesHelp.com

This book was previously published as "Legendary Customer Service" © 2022 and produced in an 8.5 x 11 size paperback book. The title, AISN, and ISBN have been changed. The publication size has also been changed to a standard 6 x 9 format. The content has remained the same.

This book is a compilation of eleven individually published customer service eBooks written by Dr. Robert DeGroot that teach how to build the necessary attitudes and skills to create legendary customer service. Seven of these books are standalone bestsellers. The list of eBooks that can be purchased separately are listed in the section entitled "Also by Robert DeGroot.

70324a

First edition

ISBN: 979-8-9908240-2-7

This book was professionally typeset on Reedsy.
Find out more at reedsy.com

Contents

Preface

Leave a Legacy of Legendary Customer Service
An Attitude and Skills-Based Approach

Introduction

What makes customer service so distinctive, eye-opening, impactful, and so good that it becomes "Legendary?"

Simple, the skilled interactions between the customer service rep and the customer that make the customer feel valued, even when problems cannot be satisfactorily resolved.

Unfortunately, we often get recordings saying, "Your call is important to us. Please remain on the line. Calls will be answered in the order in which they're received." And when we finally do get someone to help us, it's "I can't. You should have.... You'll have to.... Company policy, we no longer support that model."

Now, wait a minute. There are some top-notch companies out there with dedicated professionals who do make a difference and value their customers. And to that, I say, YES. Maybe even a handful in a lot of companies.

But the real catastrophe lies in the fact that in your own experience, you know the vast majority of companies just won't put the necessary time into training and supporting the customer interfacing staff. For the most part, it is left up to the front-line supervisor to build a team of professional-minded people who start with the right attitudes and let those right attitudes guide them in all their interactions with clients. Being genuine and sincere with unconditional positive regard for their customers and colleagues while practicing their skills is what makes good customer service legendary.

When you leave your post in customer service, what will people say about you? You can leave a legacy of supporting a team providing customer service that borders on being legendary. You can be a proud member of that team and your reputation will follow you where ever you go.

Creating Legendary Customer Service using attitudes and skills is so much less expensive than losing customer after customer or the personal toll of bearing the brunt of customer dissatisfaction. This is true, even when you cannot solve the problems that led to the interaction in the first place. The success of failure of the complaint is more about the interaction than about the ability to help the customer resolve the issue. It's more about taking care of the customer emotionally first and foremost.

Called communications or interpersonal skills, they can be clearly defined, taught, practiced, and achieve unprecedented results.

The knowledge, skills, and strategies presented in this book are based on human interaction psychology, making them applicable in many areas of life. Here, these life skills are applied to the customer service setting. Once learned, coached, and practiced, they will become second nature.

This book is a compilation of eleven customer service eBooks that provide the necessary attitudes and skills to create legendary customer service. The table of contents defines the list of eBooks that can be purchased separately.

1. Create Attitudes Instantly
2. Telephone Etiquette for Business*
3. Email Etiquette for Business *

4. Trust & Rapport Building
5. Active Listening Skills for Business*
6. Problem-Solving Model for Business*
7. Defusing Customer Anger*
8. Managing Customer Expectations*
9. Creating Customer Loyalty
10. Stress Control at Work
11. Goal Setting for Success*

*Denotes Amazon Top 100 Bestseller

eBooks 2 – 11 are also available as Web-Based Training. See https://www.saleshelp.com/ for more information.

1

Create Attitudes Instantly

Create good or bad attitudes; one word from you is all it takes!

Introduction

This short chapter teaches a very powerful single skill – the skill to instantly create attitudes.

As you'll see, it's very easy to do. It's so easy; you're already doing it – a lot. Creating attitudes in yourself, your team, and others without knowing you're doing it.

And that means if you're like most people unwittingly using this technique, it can backfire and inadvertently create bad attitudes. You get the opposite of what you want.

Can you change them? Sure. It's more complicated but doable. You'll learn four highly effective methods to undo the attitudes you unintentionally created in yourself or someone you care about.

But why does it matter? Are attitudes important?

The difference between an ordeal and an adventure is attitude – Bob Bitchin.

- Your attitude makes life a delightful wonder or a horror to endure.
- The sheer disciplining and motivating power of goal-specific attitudes is undeniable.
- A winning or losing attitude often determines the outcome for the players – win or lose.
- Value-based attitudes will determine the path you and your loved ones take in matters large and small.
- You, as a customer, have no problem knowing the attitude of the customer service person helping you. How do you feel when you sense a less than helpful attitude?
- Sellers need to help their customers create change-resistant positive attitudes about their Unique Selling Points to protect them against the onslaught of competitors trying to rip them away.

In this chapter, you will learn what you're doing now to create attitudes, how to do it better, and how to do it intentionally to help you achieve your intentions and goals. And, you'll learn how to undo the attitudes you've created that give you the opposite of what you intended.

Learn to apply this quick attitude-creating process to:

- support legendary customer service
- competitor proof your customers
- generate the disciplined mindset to win in life
- achieve self-development goals like never before
- live a longer, healthier, happier life with a smile and a sparkle in your eye
- establish guiding values for you and your family
- generate sustainable motivation through attitude strengthening

Let's get started.

Beliefs versus Attitudes

Everyone creates attitudes without knowingly doing so. What? Yes, that's right. Attitudes, good or bad, are easy to develop but difficult to change.

Beliefs are changeable when a person learns credible information that proves something different from the current belief, the belief changes to align with the new information. "I believe we should take a left up here. Nope, that's a driveway; let's go right."

Attitudes resist change regardless of the volume of credible information contrary to the belief. Ever wonder how teenagers, colleagues, or employees get some of their attitudes?

Having the right supportive attitudes when working with customers, team members, family, and friends make working with them and being around them fun and rewarding.

Identify the Attitudes You Want

So, what attitudes would you like those around you to have? In a work situation, it is equally important to know what attitudes your co-workers and direct reports think are essential for them to have. For example, in a customer service supervisor's role, you might value professionalism, rapport, respect, and integrity, and they might value friendliness, helpfulness, warmth, and care.

An unusually nasty customer having a bad day can shake our beliefs in the goodness of people. Attitudes, however, are resistant to change even in the face of significant credible contradictory information.

For sales, you might want your customers to have positive attitudes about your Unique Selling Points so they can sell internally for you when you're not around and inadvertently create objections for your competition.

For family members, you might want to instill specific attitudinal supported values that will guide their decisions throughout life.

Therefore, our objective is to convert changeable beliefs into change-resistant attitudes so they can stand the daily testing.

Creating Attitudes Formula

You create an attitude by connecting the targeted BELIEF with an EMOTION!

Creating attitudes follows the simple formula:

Belief (or Behavior) + Emotion = Attitude
B + E = A

You elicit the emotion by challenging the desired belief with some form of the question, "Why?" Asking in the form of a challenge rather than just a question of curiosity is what will elicit the defense emotions.

The challenge question "Why? " causes the person to defend the belief or behavior. **Being put on the defensive automatically elicits the DEFENSE emotions.** With the defense argument and defense emotions co-occurring, they become classically conditioned or connected, creating an attitude.

The attitude is created the moment the emotion connects to their defense logic. Challenge again, and it gets locked in deeper.

Therefore, it stands to reason that the more frequently a particular belief is challenged, the stronger the challenges become, the better they can defend them, and the stronger the attitude will be.

Take care not to overdo it. The person being challenged must win. Make the initial challenges gentle, full of curiosity, and even indirect. If necessary, help them succeed with their defense. They must win, or it backfires.

For example, for our purposes, you can use different ways to ask "why," such as "How did you come to that conclusion?" "What made you decide to do it that way?" and "When did that first become important?" It's unnecessary to initially add the emphasis in your voice that makes the challenge obvious.

One other quick point, as noted in the formula, it can be a Belief or a BEHAVIOR that you challenge. For example, if you observe them doing something you like, challenge the behavior to turn it into an attitude. You want them (and yourself) to have more robust defenses for doing the right thing than the wrong thing.

Therefore, only ask challenge-style questions about desirable beliefs or behaviors you want to see repeated more frequently with greater intensity; never, ever about undesirable behaviors.

The Formula in Action

In the 1960s social psychologist William McGuire coined the term "Attitude Inoculation" to define the procedure of creating stronger attitudes to overcome weaker ones (beliefs). By helping defeat weaker arguments for doing or not doing something (smoking, for example), the person inoculates themselves against stronger arguments, much like a weakened, partial, or dead virus is used to vaccinate you against a more potent live virus.

In the modified process you are learning here (Orient, Challenge, Support), procedural safeguards have been added for this to work in most, if not all, situations.

Challenging a belief or behavior out of the blue can elicit a negative emotion towards you for making them have to defend themselves. It starts the argument, "why are you attacking me?" That's not what you want. You must put it in a positive frame first. That's why you're supportive when you orient the person to the topic of discussion.

Use this simple process to make creating attitudes easier.

1. Orient with support
2. Challenge(s) Belief or Behavior
3. Support again

The three-step process with more explanation:

Orient the person to the targeted belief or behavior using a support sentence to bring it up for discussion, pointing it out, or catching them doing it right ("I like how you _____.").

Now, gently challenge it with the "why" question and perhaps another challenge to the response they give to your first challenge. Remember, **they must win** the defense for this to work, or it can backfire.

Finally, support it again. Support their logic and ability to explain and defend. Smile, be joyful, and exude warmth and pride in their behavior. You will connect these other emotions to the belief or behavior now becoming an attitude.

Look at these examples to illustrate the pattern used to establish attitudes. Recognize that these steps are often integrated into a more extensive dialog.

Orient with Support to the Targeted Belief or Behavior: "That's great that you like working with customers (desired belief or behavior)."

Challenge gently: "What made you want to do that?"

Let them respond. If it makes sense, you can gently challenge this response: I agree (and challenge again), "Why is that important to you?"

Support again: "I like how you decided that. It makes sense."

Orient with Support: "I like seeing you use _____ (targeted capability)."

   Challenge gently: "Why do you use it?"

   Support again: "That's important. I hadn't thought about it that way. Thank you."

Orient with Support: "Thank you for choosing to work with our company."

   Challenge gently: "What were your top reasons for choosing us?"

   You can challenge the ideas you want to be dominant.

   Support again: "I'm very pleased to hear that. Thank you. We're glad you're here."

Using the "implied' challenge, you cause the person to think about the connection between the belief or behavior and the emotion you're attaching. In this example, we'll use a positive emotion to connect to the belief and behavior.

Orient with Support: "It feels so good when you get to use your knowledge and skills to help customers." [personal experience]

   Challenge gently: Smile broadly and say, "You get that same feeling, don't you." [rhetorical question sends the challenge]

   Support again: "Yeah, that's what I'm talking about. That's why we're here." [reinforcement]

People, of course, do this to themselves all the time. It happens automatically. So, the happy feeling people get from doing something helps them want to do it again and again. They can readily defend their wanting to do it because of the good feelings it gives them. And so, helping others becomes an attitude. Many people influence our values, morals, and ethics early in life.

You could also list beliefs and behaviors that you want to become cultural attitudes for your group at work. The way to ensure this happens is to drive the challenges through all the superficial reasons, all the way to the core values that support them.

For others, we might find that we have something in common with them, and we'd like to continue developing more things in common to build a stronger rapport.

Observing them doing something we like, then asking "why" they do it, will encourage them to do it more often with greater intensity. Yes, this works with your spouse, boyfriend, girlfriend, acquaintances, children, co-workers, bosses, direct reports, and everyone else whose human.

In sales, you can use this process to competitor-proof your customer. Imagine what would happen if your decision-makers could defend your Unique Selling Points (USPs). That alone would create a lot of objections for the competitor's salesperson to have to figure out how to handle it. Once the customer can defend your USPs, they can sell for you internally when you're not around, and to decision-makers, you can't get into to see – a bonus.

Orient with Support: "I like this Feature (Unique Selling Point) because it _____ and _____. What about you?"
   Customer: "Yeah, that is nice."
   Challenge gently: It is. "Besides that, why else do you like it?"
   Customer: "It has a good _____."
   Challenge #2: "What about your boss? How do you see her liking this?"
   Customer: "Oh, she'll like _____ about it."
   Support again: "I totally agree with you on that."

If you have **children**, gently challenging them on the beliefs and behaviors that will pay off for them now and in their futures should be a daily event. Sort them out, categorize them, and boil them down to the core values you want to establish. You don't want to leave this to chance or someone else to choose which values they will adopt.

For example, when you observe them studying, compliment them on doing it, challenge them gently, help them win, then support that behavior again. Rinse and repeat until they're able to snap an emotional defense for good behavior that's strong, robust, and age-appropriate. As they grow, so must their defenses to remain age appropriate. This is how you instill values in your children. You must control which values your children adopt because they will guide them throughout their lives.

As you continue to learn the process of intentionally establishing attitudes, recognize the many times this has happened to you. Perhaps around the family dinner table, when your parents or caretaker subtly challenged your good behavior or a teacher who took particular interest in helping you along the right path challenged you to do even better.

Creating attitudes is a simple psychological process we all do. It's a life skill.

Achieving Goals with Attitudinal Support

You know what you want to achieve, but from time to time, you might not have the right attitude to make it through to the end or might not yet discover the values that will drive the goal-directed behaviors. Here, you can work with another person or by yourself to deliberately help you find these beliefs and behaviors, uncover the guiding values, and entrench the attitudes.

Orient with Support: I really want to _____.
  Challenge gently: But why?
  You defend with your reason.
  Challenge # 2: Yes, but why is that important?
  You defend your reason.
  Challenge # 3 – 10 if needed. Continue to challenge answer after answer until you feel the emotion surrounding your responses or how your answers sound.
  Support again: When you feel the "ah ha" moment with the true core answer, you'll feel a release and relief. A smile will come, and you'll know

you're done.

Remember to never, ever challenge a belief or behavior you don't want to entrench in your mind so deeply that it becomes an automatic habit of thought and act. For example, "Why can't I lose weight?" Or, "Why are you smoking?"

Instead, "Why am I ready now to lose weight?" "Why am I able to get control of my eating?" "Why do I like to exercise?" If you don't like to exercise, then you simply have to fake it until you make it. You must develop defenses about why you want it; they better be good. Keep challenging your answers until you get there. And you will. Begin now.

To the answers to these challenges, continue to drill down about each answer. Then drill down with a challenge to that answer. Continue this way until a level of emotion (perhaps frustration) gets you to the final answer—that epiphany.

Then, challenge all around that answer from many different directions and dimensions as to what it really means in all areas of your life (*personal, physical, mental, self-image, esteem, worth, emotional, spiritual, financial, professional, relationships, social, educational, etc.*).

Don't stop challenging until you have your "ah ha" defensive answer. Soak up that good feeling and associate it with the desired attitude.

Remember, for this to work, you only have to attach an emotion (pride, love, happiness, defense) to the belief or behavior, and there are many ways to do that. The quickest and easiest is using the challenge. The challenge can be direct, indirect, subtle, and even implied.

Examples of questions to drill down for more profound answers:

"And, why do I want that?"

"What is it about wanting _____ that's important to me?" "Why?"

10

"But, why that, and not something else like _____?"
"Does that sound empty to want that?"
"What does that matter to me?"
"Why now?"

Usually, the first defending responses you give will be close to what you would intellectually conclude as acceptable, rational, logical answers. Those won't get you anywhere. They won't motivate you; they won't provide the necessary discipline. You must dig deeper.

The second response is often just the opposite and is so far out there it's in "la-la" land. It's often the third, fourth, and beyond-defending responses that get you to where you want to go. They open the floodgates of the true motivating factors. You know you're there when you feel the emotion strongly or have that "ah-ha" moment. Write these down!

Don't be too surprised about what those deeper dive defensive answers say about you as a person and how they're connected to other things you'd like to change.

What about values? Identify a value and challenge yourself, challenge your response, and challenge those until you have that wonderful epiphany or the "ah-ha" experience.

This one defense may be the lead domino for you to make many helpful changes in many areas of your life. And, it might not be just one answer that gives you the epiphany. As you explore the different areas of your life where they apply, you might see the related attitudes that would strengthen your motivation.

Use the list above about the different areas of your life to see how this one answer impacts several of them.

Since you're challenging yourself in this situation and understand the purpose of linking the emotion to the belief or behavior, you can make those challenges with any degree of pressure, from gentle to confrontational.

So, imagine these defensive answers with full sensory impact: see them, hear them, touch them, taste them, smell them, feel them, sense them. Continue with this process to apply it to the other areas of your life that can be positively impacted.

Attitude Triggers

Now it's time to set the triggers that will cause the guiding attitude to drive your thoughts and behaviors. For example, a friend of mine wanted to build his stomach muscles as he lost weight. He knew that if he held his stomach in constantly, every day – as we did in the military, those muscles would build through the principle of isometrics alone. So, one of the triggers that came naturally to him was to say, "girls on the beach" with his own imagery. His reflexive response, as for most people with a few, or many, extra pounds around the waist, would be to pull the stomach in and push the chest out. Logic alone tells you this works.

Triggers can be rules. For example, "only shop around the outside perimeter of a grocery store." Why? Because that's where the fresh food is located. But fresh organic foods often cost more than the canned, processed version, you might say. Yeah, probably. So eat less. Oh yeah, that's the point. Use a smaller plate. See how you can use your trigger rules as tools to help you accomplish your goals. Learn the store layout you frequent to find what's good for you. Imagine you have blinders on as you walk down the aisle to find just what you want, seeing nothing else.

Finally, recognize if you do the behaviors in public or around friends that will get you to your goals, they might challenge you in a way that would cause you to do the opposite of what's good for you. For example, "Why don't you take the last piece." Or, "Finish your plate, or you don't get dessert." Or, "Why aren't you eating? Are you not feeling well?" "Come on, finish up." Lots of pressure, isn't there? Work on your defenses. Practice them until you feel them. Then let them bring it on.

You can continue challenging different aspects of your goal. You can identify and challenge triggers that alert you to let your value-based attitudes guide you.

Pre-plan Value-Based Attitudes

Don't leave your value-based attitudes up to chance. Select them. Define them. Challenge them. Put them on the fence to see if they can withstand the challenges. You might just surprise yourself with what's important to you and what you just thought was important. It is not uncommon to find that many of these beliefs, behaviors, attitudes, and values were important to someone else but not you. Hmm? Now that you know, you can choose.

Self-Correcting Attitudes

Have you ever done something that's not who you are and think, "Why'd I do that?" Or, "What was I thinking?" Or, "I'm so embarrassed by what I did, said, thought. How can I justify doing that?"

In the late 1950s and early 1960s social psychologist Leon Festinger developed the idea of "Cognitive Dissonance," which states that if there is a conflict between a belief and behavior, psychological tension and discomfort (i.e., cognitive dissonance) will occur. And it does.

To rid ourselves of this mental discomfort and unease, we try to come up with reasons that can help us justify what we said, did, or thought (that induced us to do some behavior inconsistent with our self-image).

And so, as you repeatedly question (challenge) yourself about a behavior, you gradually come up with reasons for doing it. Don't you? That relieves the discomfort.

But, you may still not like what you did, said, or thought. What happens next? You limit the instance to a "one-time event only." You then repeatedly find examples of the person you really are to counter this isolated instance of doing something inconsistent with your set of values.

In the end, you've justified the isolated behavior, rid yourself of the psychological discomfort, come to peace with yourself, and at the same time surrounded it with strong attitudinal evidence that your value systems are still intact, thereby making yourself feel psychologically better.

You'll see later that this process can also be used to isolate bad attitudes.

Create Bad Attitudes

"Why did you do that?!" Oops!

When it all goes wrong, people create attitudes that get the opposite of what they're trying to accomplish.

Let's get to it. When do you usually ask the "why did you do that" question? When a person does something good or bad? For example, "Why are you always late?" "Why haven't you completed your homework?" "Why (this bad behavior, or that bad belief)?

What does the person you've challenged have to defend, good behavior or bad behavior?

What's being created, good attitudes or bad attitudes?

Easy to do, isn't it? You're doing it already and have most of your life to yourself and others; they have also challenged your beliefs and behaviors. So be careful about what you challenge, or you might get the opposite of what you want.

Challenge only the beliefs or behaviors you want, and never challenge those you don't want.

"Okay, I did that. How can I fix it?"

Countering Bad Attitudes

You can counter, cover, isolate, or change "bad" attitudes in several ways. Think each of them through. You might rehearse and combine a couple of ways that work better for your interaction style. With any method you select, **always start by establishing strong rapport.** There is an other chapter in this book that will show you several methods how to it in the most trying of situations.

Creating Stronger Opposing Attitudes

One way to create counterbalancing attitudes is to wait until they exhibit the correct behavior, orient supportively, gently challenge, and help them win. Close the process by supporting them again. Rinse and repeat several times, coming from different directions.

Remember, you're taking their current attitude, no matter how strong, and deeming it the weaker one, so you can help them build a stronger one to counterbalance it.

Let's suppose the person is usually late for work. Then one day, the person shows up to work on time. Pounce. Approach, establish rapport, and then orient with support. You might say, "I really appreciate you being here on time today. We're getting slammed with customer service requests, and you know, you're one of the people I count on to get them the help they need. Next challenge. "But now I've got to ask you, how did you make it here on time?"

That's a long way around, but you get the gist of what's happening here. You've just oriented with support and challenged using the "how" question.

The person explained that they took a different route this morning. And, you say, "That was a good decision; why'd you choose that route?"

Let them respond, and then close the loop by supporting them again.

Another way to counterbalance the attitude you wish to change is to orient the discussion to related issues. For example, you might orient with support going to the movies on time. "Don't you just hate it when the movie gets to the critical opening point, and people coming in late sit down right in front of you, blocking your view?" Or, "Sorry to dump this on you, but the person relieving you on this shift hasn't shown up yet, and you'll have to stay until they do." Or, "I just wish people would be more reliable and do what they promised, like complete the reports on time! What do you think about unreliable people?"

Well, what if they never exhibit the correct behavior, or they exhibit the bad behavior again, or what if I need to change the attitude sooner than later? What now? Do it again.

Then you bring it up for discussion. For example, you might say, "Listen, I need to talk with you about something that's been bothering me and is affecting our relationship (or your relationship with the team). "Do you have time now? Or could we set an appointment to talk about it later today?"

When you begin the discussion, you orient with support to the desired Belief or Behavior and gently challenge them so they can win, just as you've done before.

"I really appreciated you being here on time yesterday, as did our customers. Let's brainstorm ways to make that a habit; what do you say? (don't pause) We know the new route you came up with worked. What are some other ideas you've been thinking about that would help?"

Let the person think about some ways. You respond by saying, "that's an idea; what's another?" Neither praising nor criticizing the idea. Ideas will flow from one extreme to another before they settle down to some real ones. This is why most managers don't start discussing selecting an idea to implement until at least the third idea is on the table.

After you have a few, let the person decide which they'll try tomorrow. "You've come up with some good ideas; how would you implement the _____? Let them think through how they would do it. It is their idea, after all. Just be sure to place the "why" challenges appropriately. For example, "I agree, and why else do you think that would work?" Let them respond; then, you can support and close with, "I can see how you'd make that one work."

Role Reversal

Another way to weaken a strong attitude toward doing bad behavior is to conduct a role reversal session. The point, counter-point debate style works well – especially with group behavior you'd like to see change. In this procedure, the person (or team) is assigned to research and develop the best arguments they can that are counter to their current attitude. At the same time, you (team B or someone you assign) should prepare to argue the person's (with a bad attitude) views, opinions, and arguments.

You can also assign sections of the attitude to different people. For example, one may argue the values that guide the behavior, while another might argue the optional behaviors and where they might lead. A lively debate is always one of the outcomes, so be prepared. You can then rotate roles in a round-robin format and repeat. This can be done in a couple of hours, or it can happen over several days.

No matter how you dress it up and talk around it, the formula is simply to Orient with Support, Challenge gently (repeatedly as needed), and then Support again. It's the rinse and repeat cycle until the right attitude gets locked in.

Surround the Target Attitude with Conflicting Attitudes

Following the "Cognitive Dissonance" idea, identify two or three beliefs or behaviors that express the same core value that counters the attitude you want to change. For example, your attitude countering strategy for coming late to work might be saying, "I know this isn't who you are. These could just be isolated times for you. But, clear something up for me. Why do you see yourself as someone on which I can rely? Why do you think I can depend on you to do what you say you will do?"

Parallel Beliefs or Behaviors

You can also surround the target attitude with more superficial and concrete beliefs or behaviors than dealing at the core values level.

For example, "If it's okay for you to be late for work, then why is it not okay for you to be late for a movie, your date, doctor, dentist, or _____?"

"If it's okay for you to embarrass others (me) when you _____, why is it not okay for them (me) to embarrass you in front of your friends by doing the same thing to you? Why is it not a good thing to intentionally embarrass _____?"

Using this reversal is a little tricky. You know the person you'll be challenging. Think about the types of answers they could throw back. If they don't defend doing the right thing, rework the question until it gets what you want.

With good rapport and a strong relationship, you can be slightly more direct and somewhat more confrontational. However, if your relationship or rapport is not as strong, or you're unsure how the person will react, I would strongly advise being gentle and less confrontational or perhaps using a different method. The short chapter "Trust and Rapport Building" might help build a stronger rapport.

Keep in mind that your emotions will already be high because you're bringing something up that already has you wound up, and the other person could take it the wrong way and feel affronted, attacked, or bad about knowing what they're doing is wrong in the first place.

Once you successfully surround the attitude you want to change with comparable but conflicting perspectives (beliefs and attitudes), it is much easier to begin directly counterbalancing the attitude to change.

Job Aid – Create Attitudes Instantly

A Belief or Behavior connected to an Emotion creates an Attitude. B + E = A

The Create Attitudes Instantly **Formula**

Belief (or Behavior) + Emotion = Attitude
  B + E = A

Process

1. Orient with support
2. Challenge(s) Belief or Behavior

3. Support again

Set Attitude Mental, Physical, and Environmental **Triggers**

Counter Bad Attitudes

- Create stronger opposing attitudes
- Role Reversal
- Surround Target Attitude with Conflicting Attitudes
- Create Parallel Beliefs and Behaviors

2

Telephone Etiquette for Business

Make positive impressions from hello to goodbye

Objectives

According to etiquette expert Letitia Baldrige, "The manner in which a company's phone is answered gives strong signals to the caller regarding the corporate character of the organization."

That's why it is essential to know how everyone in your organization answers the phone. It's not just the receptionist who answers the phone; almost everyone has a telephone on their desk, and most people talk to internal or external customers.

Telephone behavior sets customer expectations regarding your company's ability to help. The purpose of this chapter is to present telephone etiquette guidelines for anyone who interacts with customers on the phone.

These guidelines are focused on making the telephone experience positive for both parties. They will emphasize how to make the caller feel glad they called from hello to goodbye, regardless of the nature of the call.

After completing this chapter, you will have the knowledge to work within the telephone etiquette standards:

Section One: Incoming Calls

1. Maximum number of rings
2. Opening Remarks
3. Voice Tones
4. Addressing the caller

Section Two: Putting the Customer on Hold

1. What to say when putting the caller on hold
2. How long should you leave the caller on hold
3. Taking the customer off hold

Section Three: Intercom etiquette

1. Transferring a call
2. Receiving a call

Section Four: Messages

1. Taking and leaving messages
2. Don't promise what you can't deliver
3. Voicemail

Section Five: Ending the Call

· Four steps to ending the call and making them glad they called

Definitions

According to Webster's Dictionary, "etiquette" is defined as: *"The rules of behavior standard in polite society … the rules governing professional conduct."* The definition of "professional" includes *"exhibiting a courteous, conscientious, and generally businesslike manner in the workplace."*

Telephone behavior can set a positive or a negative stage for the ensuing conversation. Therefore, it is important to follow established guidelines when you represent yourself and your company over the telephone.

Section One: Incoming Calls

Maximum Number of Rings

Answer during the first three rings. The fourth ring could start to evoke negative emotions in the caller.

Why? Because when the phone isn't answered, we perceive a threat to meeting our needs. This sets us up for a potential loss. Feelings of loss trigger anger, and anger gives us the energy needed to prevent the loss. Even before we can say hello, we've got an upset customer to defuse.

Although we are becoming more accustomed to spending time in a holding queue and using menus to navigate to find help, the longer this goes on, the more it can have the same effect as time spent listening to the phone ring.

Callers begin to gauge their value to a company before the telephone is answered. The longer they have to wait for the phone to be answered, the less they think the company cares about them.

Opening Remarks

What should you say when you answer the phone? Let's start with a quick demonstration of how to embarrass the caller by just answering the phone with the company's name.

In this example, Nicky is a long-time customer of "Positive Wire Electronics," the company she's calling. She likes to engage the people she talks with; she likes the personal connection. Helen works for "Positive Wire Electronics" and occasionally answers the phone.

- Helen answers the phone, *"Positive Wire Electronics."*
- Thinking she recognizes the voice, Nicky asks, *"Is this Mary?"*
- Helen responds, *"No, this is Helen."*
- Nicky, now somewhat embarrassed, says, *"I'm sorry, you sound just like Mary."*
- Helen responds, *"That's all right."*
- Nicky now fumes and says to herself, "I hope no one in my company embarrasses our customers this way. All Helen had to do was to say her name when she answered the phone, and I'd feel much better than I do now. I'm sure this isn't the first time this has happened."

It's true. Most of us have had this less-than-pleasant experience. So how could Helen have answered the phone and not embarrassed a long-term customer?

Your opening remarks should include:

- The name of your company or department if the call has been transferred internally
- Your name
- An offer to help, "How may I help you?"
- Do this with a smile to communicate "welcome" in your voice.

Including these points in your opening enables callers to know that they dialed the correct number and are talking with someone prepared to be of assistance. Whoever answers a phone takes responsibility for that call, even if they transfer it to someone else.

You can modify these remarks with comments such as:

- *"Thank you for calling."* Or, if you're at reception or on the switchboard, you might say, *"How may I direct your call."*

· You could end with, *"I'll transfer you now, and have a wonderful day."*
· If you're in the accounting department answering a transferred call, you might say, *"Accounting department, this is Mary; how can I help you."*

Voice Tones

Your voice initially sets the entire tone of the conversation. Tired, slow-paced, annoyed, upset, or condescending voices do nothing to develop a positive cadence.

Most people get a tremendous amount of information about our value to another individual through the vocal treatment we receive. Indeed, the nuances of voice send the message rather than the words themselves.

For example:

· We can tell if the person is inexperienced by the hesitant voice quality.
· We can usually discern age, gender, and whether the person is enthusiastic about helping us or whether they consider us a nuisance.
· We prefer voices that welcome us and are understanding and helpful.
· We can also read a lot into a voice pattern that may or may not be valid.

It is essential to become aware of negative vocal behaviors and avoid them.

Creating a POSITIVE Tone of Voice

· <u>Focus:</u> Concentrate on your mission. Focus on the customer. Your sincere attention will be noticed. Put all other thoughts out of your mind except the customer's concerns.
· <u>Smile:</u> Yes, a smile can be heard over the phone. Be enthusiastic about the mission you are carrying out. A smile says, "welcome."
· <u>Sit at Attention:</u> Good posture is comfortable and can produce alert, warm

vocal overtones.

- Articulate Clearly: Use a normal volume and speak clearly. Fewer misunderstandings will be your reward.
- Positive Self-Talk: Tell yourself positive things about your ability to understand your customer's point of view, stresses, and concerns, and this will come across to the person on the other end of the phone.

Creating a NEGATIVE Tone of Voice

- Allowing Distractions: People can tell when your full attention is not focused on them. Hold a side conversation, and you will surely evoke a negative emotional response and trigger a loss of trust.
- Don't Smile: When you don't smile, your tone often sounds flat or disinterested.
- Slouch: Breathing can be affected to the extent that the power goes out of your voice.
- Slur Words: It's difficult enough to hear anything at a busy and noisy facility. With lazy speech habits, you add to anxiety, building miscommunications.
- Negative Self-Talk: What you tell yourself about the customer will most definitely come across in your tone of voice and will be reflected in your effectiveness in being of assistance.

Try this to prove it to yourself. First, sit up straight, smile, and introduce yourself out loud.

Next, let the smile fade, slouch in your chair, and introduce yourself out loud.

Notice the difference? So will your customers! Are you smiling right now?

Addressing the Caller

How you address the caller projects the level of respect, seriousness, and friendliness they will feel the call is given.

Using the more formal, Dr. Mr., Mrs., or Ms., would be appropriate when,

- The customer's corporate culture is formal
- The caller sounds older
- The caller sounds upset or sounds formal

Using first names is appropriate when

- The caller only provides the first name
- You've asked, and they agreed, or they suggest that you call them by their first names
- The caller is a peer, associate, or friend.

Some special circumstances to consider would include the society-based cultural appropriateness of using a person's name and title.

Cultural variances may be challenging to gauge. So, if a customer's name sounds quite different from what you are accustomed to, it would be best to ask for their preference. For example, you might ask, *"What would you like to be called, sir?"* Or, *"How would you like me to address you?"*

Another special situation is when the caller has a title of distinction, such as a doctor, ambassador, mayor, judge, or another similar title, then use the proper title throughout the conversation unless advised differently.

Finally, take care when using the customer's name. Repeating it too frequently can sound insincere.

Section Two: Putting the Customer on "Hold"

The hold button enables companies to handle more calls and prevents the caller from overhearing side conversations or being distracted by background noise.

Once on hold for even a brief period, the caller frequently experiences a feeling of being ignored or abandoned – especially when there is absolute silence on the line.

Consequently, hold buttons should be used sparingly. There are three etiquette guides to follow.

- What to say when putting the caller on hold
- How long to leave a caller on hold
- What to say when taking a caller off hold

What to say when putting the caller on hold

First, <u>explain the reason</u> for putting the customer on hold.
   Second, <u>ask permission</u>.
   Third, <u>wait for an answer</u>.
   Fourth, <u>push the hold button</u> before setting the receiver down.

For example:

- *"I'll be glad to look that up for you. Would you mind if I put you on hold?"*
- *"Mr. Ruiz has that information. May I place you on hold while I ask him for you?"*
- *"I'll be glad to look that up for you. Would you mind if I put you on hold?*
- *"It may take a couple of minutes; can you hold while I transfer you to customer service?"*

An exception to the asking permission guideline is when you know the person well and have a good rapport. Or you are working on a project, and you both expect to put each other on hold to complete the job. In these instances, you can simply say, *"Okay, let me put you on hold while I get that for you."*

How long to leave the customer on Hold

Don't leave a caller on hold for more than 20 seconds. If customers will be on hold for longer than 20 seconds, return to the call and let them know the process will take a few moments longer. Ask permission to leave them on hold.

If the problem will take more than two minutes, offer to call them back on or before a specified time.

Taking the customer off hold

Resume the call by **thanking the customer for waiting** or **apologizing for the inconvenience**. This allows customers to realize they weren't forgotten.

Show you care by:

- Thanking them for holding
- Apologizing for the wait

It would be helpful if you could resume the call with immediate information such as:

- *"I'm sorry you had to wait, Mr. Client. Ms. Jones is not in her office. Would you mind if I asked her to call you back? What time would be good for you?"*
- *"Thanks for holding. I've got the information you're looking for..."*

Alternately, if you are receiving a call that has been transferred to you, you might say:

- *"Mrs. Flores, thank you for holding. This is _____. May I help you?"*

NOTE: When you are given the person's name, use it in your opening remarks. It communicates organizational competence and caring to the caller. If you are unsure of the pronunciation, say it and ask if that was correct.

Section Three: Intercom Etiquette

Transferring Calls

You may have to contact someone on an intercom system in your office. For example, you may be transferring a call. Follow these guidelines for intercom etiquette:

- Place the caller on hold before you use the intercom.
- *"Ms. Smith, I will transfer you to Mr. Jose Garcia at extension 123. Can you hold?"*
- Use the appropriate procedure for your phone system and connect to the phone of the person you are trying to reach.
- Do not announce yourself or call their name just in case they are on the phone or in a meeting. Virtually all modern phones will beep or ring to announce the intercom connection.

Depending on your system type, you may hear the same tone they hear. Once the connection is made, you are on an open mike on their intercom. You can listen to what is being said in their office, so do not disturb them. They know you are there, so do not announce yourself or call their name. Having said that, some people will ask you to announce yourself.

For example, *"Ms. Jones, this is Carla. I have a call holding for you."* Wait for them to let you know if they are available or not. The general guideline is that the person being called is responsible for speaking first.

They should say their name and make an offer to help. The rule is always to be polite and professional. The person may be in the outer office hearing everything you say.

When transferring a call, let the person know who is calling and what the call is about. That way, the caller doesn't have to re-explain why they are calling. If not, be brief to minimize the time the caller is on hold.

Receiving an intercom call

When you hear the tone, say your name and make an offer to help. It's your responsibility to respond to the intercom first. Don't expect the person on the other end to interrupt you more than the tone did.

Be sure to get the name of the person being transferred to you (confirm the spelling as needed) and ask the purpose of the call so that you can be prepared to take it.

Section Four: Messages

Taking or leaving message

If the person being called is unavailable, it may be necessary to take a message for them. The quality of the message can have a direct impact on the results of the callback.

Of course, with voicemail, callers can leave their messages. Yet, often, it is necessary to take a message. A message must provide sufficient information to prepare the recipient to make the return call. You may have to ask the caller for this information.

Getting or giving the correct information:

"I keep six honest serving-men, (They taught me all I knew); Their names are What and Why and When, And How and Where and Who" - Rudyard Kipling

When you are taking a message or leaving a "voicemail" message, the primary information to consider is:

1. WHO called? (spell name)
2. WHAT did they want? (action)
3. WHEN did they call? (time, date, and when to call back)
4. WHERE did they call from? (company, department, city)
5. HOW do I contact them? (phone number(s) for call back)
6. WHY now? (urgency)

Before hanging up, it's a good idea to read the message back to the caller to ensure that you have all the information written correctly and ask for the best time(s) for the call to be returned.

Don't promise what you can't deliver

When taking a message, take care that you don't promise the caller something you can't deliver.

For example, it would not be wise to tell a caller that you will have someone return the call as soon as they arrive. Instead, it would be better to tell the caller that you will give the person the message and let them know about its urgency.

See the difference? You can't physically make someone return a call, but what you can do is "ask" them to return the call.

Voicemail

With voicemail, callers leave their messages. Your job then may simply be to transfer the person to voicemail. For example, *"Mr. Smith is out of the office today. Would you like to leave a message on his voicemail?"*

Leaving a voicemail:

Of course, you should always be prepared to leave a message. Before you call, you should know the who, what, when, where, why, and how of your own communication.

When you're leaving a voicemail message for someone who does not know you, say your name clearly at the beginning of the message. You will also repeat it at the end of the message.

If your name can be confusing to understand and to say, develop and use a simple memory device such as rhyming or associating it with something commonly known and recognizable.

Also, say your phone number clearly at the "beginning" of the message and twice again at the end of the message.

Say it slowly and clearly. If the numbers can be misunderstood, then repeat them differently. For example, you could say 5, 5, 9, 9, and then, fifty-five, ninety-nine. That's much clearer now, isn't it?

Your own voicemail box should say:

- Your name - Pronounce it slowly and clearly.
- Your status - *"I am out of the office until _____."*
- Your backup (if available) - *"If you need to speak with someone before then, please get in touch with Theresa Jones at 281-333-5555, extension 22. If not,*

then please leave a message. Thank you."
- Say the backup person's name and number slowly. Repeat if necessary.

Section Five: Ending the Call

When you contact someone who loves to talk, it can become challenging to complete the telephone call gracefully once you've finished your business transaction.

It is unacceptable to simply hang up on a customer who won't stop talking. And, it doesn't feel good to them when someone says they have to go now.

The following process can be used in these situations to help you successfully end the call and make the customer feel glad they called.

Four Steps to End the Call

1. Use the caller's name.
2. Review accomplishments using the past tense.
3. State next steps.
4. Verify all concerns have been addressed.

Let's take a closer look at each step.

Step 1. Use the caller's name. People pay attention when they hear their name being spoken, which is an excellent way to interrupt to get their attention without risking offending them. It also signals that something important is about to be said.

Step 2. Review what you've accomplished on this call in a positive way using the past tense. This starts them thinking in terms of the call being over.

Step 3. State the next steps. This confirms that both you and the customer understand what will happen next. Note particularly any action items that must be completed by either you or the customer, when they will be done, and any follow-up that will be required.

Step 4. Verify that all concerns have been addressed. This clearly signals that this part of the call is at an end and brings them back on track if other issues need to be addressed.

Here is an example of the four steps in action:

1. *"Okay, Mr. Jarvis..."*
2. *"Let me sum up what we've done. I've taken the information you provided and completed the order entry, and I just sent it to the appropriate department for processing."*
3. *"What will happen next is that you'll receive the confirmation paperwork from us in a few days, and your order should arrive within a week. I think we've completed that item."*
4. *"Is there anything else I can help you with today?"*

Summary Checklist of Skills

Section One: Incoming Calls

Number of rings = 3 Max

- Answer before the fourth ring

Opening Remarks

- Your company or department name
- Your name
- Offer to help

Positive Voice Tones

- Focus
- Smile
- Good posture
- Articulate clearly

- Positive Self-Talk

Addressing the caller

- Use formal Dr. Mr., Mrs., or Ms., when:
- Corporate culture
- The caller sounds older or upset
- As indicated by title or corporate culture
- Use first names when:
- The caller only provides the first name
- You ask, and they agree
- They suggest
- The caller is a peer, associate, or friend
- Special Circumstances
- Society-based cultural variances, then ask how they would prefer to be addressed
- Use Titles of Distinction (mayor, judge, ambassador)
- Repeating name too often sounds insincere

Section Two: Putting the caller on hold

What to say when putting the caller on hold

- Explain why, and ask permission
- Wait for an answer and acknowledge it
- Push the hold button

How long should you leave a caller on hold?

- 20 Seconds Max
- Return to call every 20 seconds to ask for more time if needed
- Or, if more than 2 minutes, offer to call them back

Taking the customer off hold

- Thank the customer for holding
- Or, Apologize for the wait
- Transferred call? Use the customer's name

Section Three: Intercom etiquette

Intercom Etiquette - Transferring

- Place the caller on hold
- Connect to the person
- Do not disturb - they heard the tone
- Wait for them to speak first

Intercom Etiquette – Receiving

- Say your name
- Make an offer to help
- Get the name of the person calling
- Get the purpose of the call

Section Four: Messages

Messages – taking and leaving (5 "W's" + 1 "H")

1. Who called?
2. What did they want?
3. When did they call?
4. Where did they call from?
5. Why should I contact them?
6. How do they want me to contact them?

Section Five: Ending the Call

Ending the Call Steps

1. Use the caller's name
2. Review accomplishments using the past tense
3. State next steps
4. Verify all concerns addressed

Telephone Etiquette guidelines are simple, logical, professional, and essential. You represent your organization when you take or place a call, and the caller's perception of you and your organization is up to you.

Job Aid – Telephone Etiquette

INCOMING CALLS
- ❏ Answer before the 4th ring
- ❏ Strong positive greeting:
- ◆ Company Name ◆ Your Name, ◆Offer to help ◆ smile
- ❏ Address the customer by name

USING HOLD
- ❏ Ask for permission, wait for the response, and press hold
- ❏ 20 seconds maximum. If longer, ask for more time or offer to call back
- ❏ Back online – thank or apologize for the wait

INTERCOM ETIQUETTE

- · Put the caller on hold ◆ connect ◆ wait for the response
- · Announce caller by name and purpose of the call.

MESSAGES – Taking or Leaving

- Who ◆ What ◆ When ◆ Where ◆ Why ◆ How

ENDING CALL GUIDELINES

- Use caller's name ◆ Review accomplishments using past tense ◆ State next steps ◆ Verify all concerns addressed

3

Email Etiquette for Business

Know the differences between business and personal email

Objectives

Today email is a routine part of how we communicate and document much of what we do at work. It is not uncommon for people who "text" a lot for personal use to mix up what is appropriate for work versus what's appropriate for personal use.

With so many people using email for business purposes, guidelines have been established to prevent poor manners or misuse from tarnishing business relationships.

After completing this chapter, you will know to:

- Define the purpose of business email "etiquette."
- Know if email is the correct communication vehicle
- Understand limits to confidentiality
- Understand the use of disclaimers
- Understand the permanency of email
- Know how to structure the message for business purposes
- Know how to use information such as addresses, cc's, subjects, and

signature lines
- Use "plain text" or "HTML" format as appropriate
- Know when and when not to use "emoticons" and abbreviations
- Develop an Email thread and know when to start a new one
- Know what to forward and what not to forward

Definitions

Electronic mail, commonly known today as "email," uses the Internet to send messages to one or more people.

In addition to being a standard communication method, email can be used to:

- Strengthen professional image through the use of businesslike language
- Enhance efficiency with concise writing
- Provide rapid response to pressing business issues
- Enable time for thoughtful communications to customers and others with more sensitive inquiries
- Provide a paper trail to document communications

Your company's image of professionalism can be influenced by how you conduct your email communications.

Email has an immediacy about it and consequently sets expectations of a quick response. People in business expect a response within 24 hours. This could be compared with "text" messaging, which carries the expectation of getting a reply in a few minutes or less. Instant messaging has the expectation that the response will be immediate.

Email Versus _____?

There are several ways to communicate other than email. For example:

- Telephone
- Text
- Instant messengers
- Video chat
- Fax
- Postal service
- Overnight Letter
- Courier
- In-person

Reasons to choose email include:

- Rapid communication
- Immediate interaction is not needed
- Important to document messages
- Not an emotionally loaded topic
- Minimal risk of being misunderstood
- Meeting in person is not necessary
- Can be supported with other communications as needed

Email is NOT Confidential

In reality, **email is not confidential** in the sense you would like it to be!

Employers have the right to know what is being communicated on their behalf. In addition, courts of law can subpoena your email under certain circumstances. Always remember that once you send it, you lose absolute control of it. As we'll see in the next section, disclaimers can help.

Also, be aware that an email can unintentionally be written to become a legal agreement. Be sure you are saying what you want to say. **This is not**

legal advice in this book, and only a duly qualified attorney can provide that for you.

I hope you can now see why it's essential that you know, understand, and **follow your company's "email policy."**

Since what you say in your email can be reviewed by others, you may want to **adopt a diplomatic style.** It's wise to be courteous in all communications - especially written ones!

The first time you accidentally send something questionable to the wrong person and get "flamed" (get yelled at with highly inflammatory statements in a reply email), you know you're walking a very thin line that could be costly to you and your employer.

Disclaimers

Since emails are not confidential, companies can ask that you include a "disclaimer" in the "signature" area. The disclaimer attempts to let an accidental recipient know what to do with it and what they shouldn't do.

Disclaimers are essential to those in positions of routinely transmitting sensitive information via email (attorneys, human resources, insurance agents, etc.). However, recognize that using disclaimers on every email may reduce its importance and strength.

Examples of Disclaimers:

1. This email and any attachments transmitted with it are confidential and solely for the intended recipient's use. If you were not the intended receiver, please contact the sender immediately and delete this message and attachments. Do not distribute, copy, or print it. Thank you for your cooperation.

2. THE INFORMATION CONTAINED IN THIS EMAIL MESSAGE IS IN-TENDED ONLY FOR THE USE OF THE INDIVIDUAL OR ENTITY NAMED ABOVE. IF THE READER OF THIS MESSAGE IS NOT THE INTENDED RECIPIENT, YOU ARE HEREBY NOTIFIED THAT ANY DISSEMINATION, DISTRIBUTION, OR

COPYING OF THIS COMMUNICATION IS STRICTLY PROHIBITED.

Note that disclaimers are sometimes written in red so that the reader rarely misses them.

If the message and attachments are particularly sensitive or confidential, it would seem wise to put the notice of confidentiality at the beginning of the message, before the person reads it, rather than at the end, after the fact.

In the opinion of one business attorney, "The unintended recipient has already read the text of the email before he sees the disclaimer. It would be better if the disclaimer appeared before the message's text. Also, if you claim every email is confidential, even those that are clearly not confidential, it becomes much harder to successfully assert that an email really intended to be sent in confidence is a "confidential" email."

In addition to the confidentiality disclaimer, there are many other types as well. For example, some are written to protect companies against unintentional transmission of viruses, while others protect against unintended contracts.

Laws that govern written communications regarding copyright, defamation, discrimination, and harassment also apply to email. Take care, or your message could be seen on the bulletin board, published in the local newspaper, or read to you by the plaintiff's attorney in a court of law!

Separate opinion from fact and be clear about which is which in your writing.

Errors of fact tend to diminish your reputation as a knowledgeable person. Even minor mistakes, particularly those said with emotion (flame), will discredit you and make your judgment questionable.

It's wise to be courteous in all communications - especially written ones!

Can others access your email program? Sometimes, it might not be wise to leave your email account open when you leave your computer. Others may use it to send messages for which you could be held accountable.

Plain Text or HTML

Selecting the settings on your email program has most likely been taken care of by your IT department.

You need to know if you are using "Plain Text" or "HTML."

Plain Text: Sometimes, you will receive an email with no formatting. When you select to reply, you will notice that you cannot add any formatting such as bold or italics with these types of emails. This is because the email is in "Plain Text."

Plain text does not allow you to bold, use italics, or other text formatting capabilities found in HTML

In place of italics, you would typically use them for book names, newspapers, or quoted statements. With earlier minimal Plain Text, you can use the underscore or the asterisk instead of quotation marks or italics.

HTML: HTML enables you to use bold and italics and other formatting capabilities, including inserting tables, audio, animations, and even movies into the body of the message.

If you send an email in HTML and it is received by someone using Plain Text, all the formatting will be lost. Even now, a surprisingly large number of people use Plain Text email programs or have their email program set to Plain Text. Test your business email to ensure it will work in both HTML and Plain Text. That means using advanced formatting when you know the recipient can view it.

If you see Plain Text in an original or reply email, you know to plan for Plain Text when communicating with this person.

Top & Bottom Information

To, cc, bcc, subject & signature lines

To: Most companies set up email addresses following a format for everyone. Your email at work follows your company's format. See examples of different formats.

Always double-check whom you selected to receive the email. It's not uncommon to accidentally choose someone above or below the targeted person on a list. Auto-fill can sometimes really trip you up. I guess that's when you'll be glad you had a disclaimer in your email.

Cc: cc means "carbon copy." This is a holdover expression from the days of the typewriter when carbon paper was used to make copies.

Copy someone when:

- They are not going to be asked to take on an action item
- It makes sense for them to be kept up to date on the information
- If they were going to be asked to take some action, they would be listed in the "To:" field

Bcc: Blind copy someone (bcc) when:

You are sending a message to a list of people, and they haven't given you permission to broadcast their email addresses. Put everybody in the bcc field. Put your address in the "to" field.

Subject line: Ask yourself how this email should be filed or what topic people would typically use to search for this email. This tells you what to use to write a searchable single topic or "subject" that identifies the content.

So, this subject must both identify the email's content and provide an intuitive topic to use for searching.

Signature lines: Signature lines can clearly identify yourself and your business affiliation. They can provide additional identifying information such as title or department and other contact information such as phone or fax numbers. Use 3 to 5 lines maximum

If you work from home, do not include your home address. You do not want someone looking at your home from a mapping program close-up satellite view.

Do not include "sayings" or quotes unless it's a part of your business.

And, unless it is part of your company's identifying marks, do not use fancy fonts or colors. Oh, and by the way, do not use a wallpaper background on your business emails.

For example,

Bob DeGroot
Sales Training International
281-367-5599
www.SalesHelp.com

Business Email Layout

As in any business letter, there is a salutation, a message, and a closing.

However, in email, the message is often somewhat brief and includes the use of bulleted and numbered lists, with any call for action set off to be clear.

Since you think faster than you can type or copy, cut, and paste words, phrases, and sentences, proofreading email messages is an absolute must!

Salutations: Use formal and informal greetings as indicated by the situation, tone, and level of rapport. For example, "Dear Mr. Garcia" or "Hello Juan" would be appropriate under the right circumstances.

The first email to a person you do not know well should follow the more formal salutations: Mr., Mrs., Ms., Dr., or Miss.

If two or more people are getting the same message and all their names are being used, then all the salutations should have the same formality. Select the person at the most formal level as the model to use for all. For example, if one person is addressed as Mr. or Mrs., all the people should be addressed with the same salutation.

When you get a reply email from someone, you can see how they sign their name and with a growing rapport, use that in your salutation except:

- When this is a person by stature, position, or other reason you would use a more formal salutation, it may be appropriate to continue using it.
- Standard usage in a peer-to-approximate peer is to use first names without the "Dear" in the salutation.

Language formality: Use "businesslike" language. You might be more casual with a colleague, but what if that person forwards your email to a client?

- Reading from the screen is more difficult than reading from paper, so use short sentences (15 to 20 words).
- Keep email messages short - 5 or fewer brief paragraphs. If there is a lot of content, it might be better to put that in an attachment and reference it in the email itself.
- Get to the point quickly.
- Use short paragraphs and write them as succinctly as possible.
- When making points use numbers or bullets.
- Spell months to avoid confusion, e.g., August 12, 2014, verses 8 − 12 − 22. Or is that 12/8/2022 (European and most of the world), or did you mean 08/12/2022 (USA)?
- Action Items should be clearly identified.
- Use uppercase only when making important points, headings, or titles in "Plain Text" email; otherwise, it's considered "SHOUTING."
- Your grammar, spelling, and punctuation determine the message's readability.

- Use your software's "spell checker" and "grammar checker" capabilities. Set your email options so that all messages are checked automatically before sending.
- Proofread again. And good manners suggest that you will never criticize another person's failure to proofread.

Emoticons and Emojis: Emotions are often expressed using "emoticons." Emoticons are these little sideways faces made with characters from the keyboard, such as ":-)." Emojis are the graphic versions.

Emojis are acceptable in personal emails but are not usually appropriate for business emails. However, there are times when rapport is strong, and a note could be considered negative; then, it might work. Having said that, it would be better to state the intention, such as, "I'm saying this with high humor."

Abbreviations: As in a standard business letter, state the content during the first use and then put the abbreviation in parenthesis immediately following. For example, the Association for Talent Development (ATD) or Sales Training International (STI).

In the Internet world, people do what they can to economize keystrokes. This is a habit left from the days of minimal space and minimal bandwidth. However, unless you know the person you are writing to understands these rapidly becoming archaic abbreviations, it would probably be best to avoid them.

However, common abbreviations are appropriate when you're limited to time and space, especially when "texting." Here are some of the more common abbreviations:

- Be seeing you: BCNU
- By The Way: BTW
- For What It's Worth: FWIW

- For Your Information: FYI
- In My Humble Opinion: IMHO
- Ta Ta For Now: TTFN
- Talk To You Later: TTYL
- Laughing out loud: LOL

Appearance – Fonts, Colors, and Wallpaper: The default font size is 10 points. Large font sizes are as irritating as tiny sizes. 10 - 12 points are the sizes to use.

Avoid colors other than dark blue or black. Light shade text on a dark background can be challenging to read, especially on a smartphone. Red is acceptable on necessary disclaimers.

Wallpaper, unless issued by your company, while very acceptable for personal email, it is not appropriate for business emails.

Multi-topic messages

For clarity and brevity, try to use only single-topic messages. However, when you have multiple topics, find a subject that covers all topics and use it.

Use a basic "e-Newsletter" format in which the sub-topics are listed and numbered; each is listed, numbered, and discussed.

If using Plain Text, the headings should be done in all caps.

Multi-Topic Email Example:

Opening remarks go in the first sentence. Then list the topics:

1. First topic
2. Second topic

1. THE FIRST TOPIC TO TALK ABOUT: All caps are used here when using "Plain Text" format to make it stand out and easy to find. With HTML, you can use "bold." Now provide information about the topic.

ACTION ITEM: If there is an Action Item, it too should be in all caps in Plain Text or bolded in HTML

2. THE SECOND TOPIC TO TALK ABOUT: Next, provide the content for this topic.

ACTION ITEM: If none, state so here.

Read Receipts

Read Receipt and Delivery Receipt is something you can ask your software to do by checking the appropriate boxes.

However, in general, this is not a good thing to do. It sends the message that you're checking up on them to find out if they opened your email.

If you're going to use Read Receipts, let the person know that you will use this to make sure a particularly important message got to them, so they don't have to reply.

Attachments

Take care with attachments, especially large ones.

The recipient's server sometimes rejects attachments over five megs. Ask for size restrictions if you must send a large attachment.

Any attachment must be necessary to the subject matter of the email.

Threads

A thread is a continuous flow of thought and conversation where the previous related emails are included. This is accomplished by using the "Reply All" feature.

The advantages of using threads are multiple and include:

- ease of tracking previous conversations
- ease of refreshing personal knowledge of the discussion
- ease of bringing someone new into the thread and bringing them up to speed

As long as the topic remains the same, continue to use the same thread. When the topic changes, it's appropriate to start a new thread.

On occasion, threads become much more relaxed and informal. A word of caution - don't become so casual that sensitivities are ignored; or, the next thing you know, someone is being "flamed."

Here's an example of a thread. Note that the earliest message is at the bottom.

— — -Original Message— — -
From: Kim Hammer [mailto: Kim.Hammer@ourco.com]
Sent: Tuesday, November 09, 2004, 4:30 PM
To: DeGroot, Bob
Subject: RE: Online shipping documents

Hi Bob,

Pam says, "thanks for the quick turnaround" you and your programmers did on uncovering the shipping document issue for Mr. Hank.

See Pam's comments below.

I see on the schedule that you're in tomorrow. Please give me a call early in the morning. I'd like you to walk me through how to look up customers' shipping charges with the new forms you launched.

Thanks

Kim

Kim Hammer
  Senior Tech Consultant
  (800) xxx-0000 Ext 4110
  OurCo Inc
  www.OurCo.com

——-Original Message——-
  From: Runhill, Pam [mailto: Pam.Runhill@ourco.com]
  Sent: Tuesday, November 09, 2004, 2:57 PM
  To: Hammer, Kim
  Subject: RE: Online shipping documents

Hi Kim,

Thanks for the good news, and let David know that I appreciate him being able to get back as quickly as he did.

I'll let Tom know immediately. He's really a great customer.

Thanks,

Pam

Customer Service Manager
  (800) xxx-xxxx Ext 4100
  OurCo Inc
  www.OurCo.com

———-Original Message———-
  From: Kim Hammer [mailto: Kim.Hammer@ourco.com]
  Sent: Tuesday, November 09, 2004, 2:20 PM
  To: Runhill, Pam
  Subject: RE: Online shipping documents

Hello Pam,

I talked with David in the IT department, and it appears that the programmers were in the process of updating the online forms at the same time Mr. Hank submitted his data. Evidently, the timing was unfortunate for Mr. Hank, and that issue has been resolved. With the new form, they also took care of the problem of being able to go back and fill in blank spaces (or edit current information) without having to complete a new form.

You can let Tom Hank know that the server error message has been resolved, and his shipment is being sent just as he entered the order. Other customers should not get the error message.

Kim

Kim Hammer
  Senior Tech Consultant
  (800) xxx-0000 Ext 4110
  OurCo Inc
  www.OurCo.com

———-Original Message———-

From: Runhill, Pam [mailto: Pam.Runhill@ourco.com]
Sent: Tuesday, November 09, 2004, 1:06 PM
To: Hammer, Kim
Subject: RE: Online shipping documents

Any update on why this occurred? Many of our customers will be in the system, and I am concerned that the error will continue to pop up without resolution, causing confusion.

I've sent a message to Tom Hank letting him know we're working on it and should be back to him soon.

Thank you.

Pam Runhill
   Customer Service Manager
   (800) xxx-0000 Ext 4100
   OurCo Inc
   www.OurCo.com

——-Original Message——-
   From: Kim Hammer [mailto: Kim.Hammer@ourco.com]
   Sent: Monday, November 08, 2004, 9:45 AM
   To: Runhill, Pam
   Subject: RE: Online shipping documents

Pam -

I am checking on this problem. As Tom noted, all his info was saved. I will email you the resolution.

Yours,

Kim

Kim Hammer
  Senior Tech Consultant
  (800) xxx-0000 Ext 4110
  OurCo Inc
  www.OurCo.com

——-Original Message——-
  From: Runhill, Pam [mailto: Pam.Runhill@ourco.com]
  Sent: Sunday, November 07, 2004, 8:14 PM
  To: Hammer, Kim
  Subject: FW: Online shipping documents

Kim,

Can you look at this and determine why this error occurred? Also, please verify that the system accepted Tom's information. Tom is a long-time customer, and I would like to get back to him as quickly as possible. Please provide an update to me by noon tomorrow.

Thanks.

Pam
  Customer Service Manager
  (800) xxx-xxxx Ext 4100
  OurCo Inc
  www.OurCo.com

——-Original Message——-
  From: Hank, Tom
  Sent: Sunday, November 07, 2004, 5:48 PM
  To: Dunhill, Pam

Subject: Online shipping documents

Pam,

I completed the online shipping documents. When I hit the "submit" button, I got an error message indicating a server problem. I went back to the documents, and my information was all still there. Can you tell if the system accepted my information?

Tom Hank

Business Manager
  Your Best Customer, LLC
  Tel: (800) xxx-0000

Reply All

When you select "Reply All," everyone is included. If you need to work with just one person as a part of the project, do not select "Reply All." Under these circumstances, starting a new thread with the appropriate person would be best so that as you report to the larger group, the main thread is still intact.

Don't "Reply All" just to say "Thanks." You can use "Reply" to address a single individual to say "Thanks."

Email software set for "Plain Text" uses the ">" symbol to mark previous emails and continues to add a right carrot ">" upon each additional sending. So, it is possible to get several of these marks "»»»."

Email software set for HTML function allows you the option to include the previous message and indent or not indent. You can also choose not to include previous messages, but that would defeat the purpose of the thread.

If the thread is long, take off the "indent" selection, or soon you will find that the earlier messages become unreadable.

Deleting Emails

Keep old emails to a minimum. **If your company has a policy regarding what should be kept and filed, follow this to the letter.**

In general, clear out (delete) old non-relevant emails. Compressed and archived as they are, they can reach gigabyte size based on the sheer volume of emails sent and received by a single individual. This is especially true with people who deal with large attachments.

Keep only the correspondence you would ordinarily file if it came by snail mail, such as necessary documentation regarding a project - especially any that authorize work, billing, materials shipping, and so on.

Be careful when deleting emails that contain a complete thread. Be sure you are through with it and won't need it in the future. If the possibility exists that you will need it, then file it accordingly so that it will be archived for future reference if needed.

Out of Office Message

If you will be out for any length of time, set up an "Out of Office" automatic reply to emails you may get while you're out. It lets customers know why you haven't responded.

For example, "I am out of the office starting the week of February 09 and will return February 20. If you require immediate assistance, please contact Blanch DeGroot at Blanch@saleshelp.com or call customer service at xxx-xxx-xxxx. Thank you, Bob."

Be sure to remove it upon your return.

Final Tips

To Forward or Not to Forward: Don't send jokes. Others may not have the same sense of humor as you.

- Don't get involved with chain letters; they burn time and consume bandwidth.
- Do not forward emails containing any content that is sexually oriented, libelous, defamatory, offensive, racist, or obscene (graphic or text).
- Hoax and virus alerts should not be forwarded. Contact IT admin and advise them of the situation; they will know the proper protocol for your company. If none is available, look it up on Semantic.com, McAfee.com, or Snopes.com to determine the appropriate course of action.

To Flame or Not to Flame: Email can sound harsh, stupid, or even inflammatory from certain writers. Give them the benefit of the doubt.

- Don't respond when you're angry. Your emotion will come out in your writing. With this, you might start a "Flame" thread that is destructive to all involved. Flaming someone is to express in email anger or other negative sentiments toward them in no uncertain terms. Not good form!
- Do not send an email when you are angry.
- If you compose an email angrily, the message's intent will be overshadowed by emotion.
- Once it is sent, you cannot retrieve it. In hindsight, you may see overreaction when you reread your email, but it is too late to mend fences.
- If you react when angry, hold the email for 24 hours and reread it before sending it. This will allow you to gain perspective and revise the email before sending it.

Calendar - Keep it up to date: Co-workers need to know when you're available and when you're not.

- Check the calendar before sending a customer to a co-worker to ensure they're not out for the next few days.

Summary Checklist

Considering just the email itself, here is a quick summary of items to consider.

- Proper salutation: In the Salutation, did you address him as "Mr. Bender?" This would be the recommendation if he used the salutation when introducing himself.
- A polite first line such as, "Thank you for your order you placed with us, and here is the contact information for our Accounts Receivable department."
- Diplomatic presentation of potentially sensitive information: "I've copied Ms. Sally Jones so that she will recognize your request and payment when she sees it coming in without the actual statement enclosed."
- State or list action items, if any.
- Proofread for spelling, grammar, and style: Did you proofread your email before you selected send?
- Note that spell check would take place automatically when you select "send" if that option was selected in your "Tools/Options" setup.
- Proofread for unintentional "abruptness." Warm and personable with a reasonable degree of business formality, without being overly friendly, is difficult to master style but pays dividends when achieved. [Hint: Save and study emails that accomplish this goal to understand that style.]
- Offer further assistance in your closing remarks.
- Close with your regards and contact information in your signature lines.

Example: Best regards. Sincerely, Warm regards, etc.

Sally

Ms. Sally Jones
  Supervisor, Accounts Receivable
  OurCo. Inc.
  1200 Center Drive
  Anytown, TX 77380
  Phone (281) xxx-1111

Summary

I hope you've enjoyed this short chapter about Business Email Etiquette. You only need to look at a sampling of the emails you get every day to see just how important this topic is to the image of your organization.

Job Aid - Email Etiquette

SALUTATIONS
  ❏ Mr., Mrs., Ms., Miss, Dr. ❏ Stature ❏ Address themselves ❏ Tone of conversation

LANGUAGE

- Business like
- Short sentences
- Short paragraphs
- Spell "months" (June 5 versus 6/5)
- Get to the point quickly
- Highlight Action Items
- Upper case = YELLING
- SPELL CHECK
- PROOFREAD
- Diplomatic, Courteous

- Bullet or number lists

TIPS

- No :-)
- Spell out before Abbreviating
- Color: Black, Blue & Company
- Read receipts need prior warning
- Use 10 - 12-point font
- Subject – easy to file
- Double-check "To" name and address
- cc/bcc right people
- Respect threads

4

Trust and Rapport Building

Five Methods to Rapidly Build Trust and Rapport

Objectives

The purpose of this chapter is to present a straightforward means of establishing trust and rapport with customers. The content is directed to customer service personnel, sales personnel, and people in customer service roles who are also responsible for sales.

- Define trust as it relates to customers.
- Define rapport and how it impacts customer attitudes and behaviors.
- Differentiate between motive and technique.
- Recognize the importance of the customer's four business needs.
- Recognize methods that create and strengthen trust and rapport in a business setting.
- Describe the concept of Psychological Truth.
- Definitions

By understanding the meaning of "trust" and the meaning of "rapport," you will be able to understand better why some things you say and do create trust while others break or block it.

Trust: Belief without proof

Trust is measured by the level of confidence a person has in predicting the actions of others in a specific situation. The more someone is like us in language, dress, attitudes, and other factors, the more we feel we can predict their behavior. This prediction is based on understanding how we might respond to a similar event.

Rapport: Harmony

Caring about a person and focusing on them creates an attraction, becoming a connection that helps tune and synchronize attitudes, values, and trust. You begin to talk at the same pace with the same intonations, and your postures adjust to each other. As "rapport" builds, you become more like the other person, and they become more like you. As harmony (similarities) grows, so does trust. Rapport lays the foundation for trust to occur.

Motivation versus Technique

Think about the last telemarketing call you got. When you picked up the phone, could you tell if the person was trying to sell you something? Could you tell if that person really cared about what they were selling?

Can you hear a smile over the phone? Of course, you can. Smiling changes your voice tones and rhythm.

Check your mindset. The customer will. The customer will know whose needs you're trying to fill, no matter what your technique is.

Stay focused on helping the customer meet the needs fulfilled by your product or service.

Five Methods to Establish Trust & Rapport

Five standard methods to explore:

1. Common Ground
2. Pacing & Leading

3. Credentials
4. Brochures
5. Psychological Truth

Common Ground

Common ground can be anything that you share in common. It can be an interest or experience. How do you discover this common ground? You do it with "small talk." Start with open-ended questions, "How do you like this weather we're having?"

Safe topics for establishing common ground include:

- Weather
- Distance from work
- Traffic
- Current events
- Education
- Work experiences
- Places

Topics to avoid:

- Religion
- Politics
- Sports – sometimes a very sensitive topic.

In general, anything that has "sides" or is sensitive or controversial should be avoided.

Pacing & Leading

Pacing means to mirror and match a characteristic of another person. The pacing process is to observe the person, then approximately match the behavior to "connect."

Example: If you're a fast walker and your client walks slower unless you change your pace to match his/hers, you will soon be walking alone.

Pacing exists in:

- Language – speed, tone, cadence
- Posture – sitting, standing
- Dress – business, formal, beach
- Emotion – show empathy and appropriate intensity but don't pace negative emotions

Don't pace profanity or any other inappropriate behavior.

Leading is once connected, you can then change the pace, and the other person will follow.

For example, talk a little faster/slower, or sit up straight, lean forward/back. The person who wants the conversation to occur is the one who initially paces the other.

Credentials

Credentials tell customers that you are a professional interested in helping them fill their needs. Credentials can include:

- A title that defines your area of expertise
- An affiliation with a capable company
- A referral from a respected source
- An applicable knowledge or experience

- A professional appearance and behavior

Trust is passed between you and your company. If customers trust you, they will most likely transfer that trust to your company and vice versa.

Credentials build positive expectations. Your title tells the customer of your profession. Your company name and reputation can support positive expectations.

Credentials build credibility. Track records, testimonials, references, and client lists talk about your capabilities and performance standards.

Credentials build power. Few people go to those who appear weaker than they are for help. We usually seek strong people to help us get what we need.

Take a moment to think about the credentials you bring to your job. Jot them down. Think again about why they are important to the customer. What added value do your credentials bring to the customer?

Brochures

Brochures and other printed collateral materials impact the customer in at least four major ways:

- If it's in print, it must be true.
- It must be of value if it's in pristine condition (no marks or bent pages).
- Sales literature should be working literature.
- The respect you show your collateral materials will directly influence the value the prospect gives what it represents.

Always ensure the prospect gets the "corporate image" brochure if you have them. It tends to raise the level of trust by creating an association in the customer's mind with you and the prestige shown in the brochure.

Sales literature (different from marketing literature) is usually more detailed about the features, advantages, and benefits of a particular product or service.

People in decision-making positions receive sales literature and brochures every day. It is not surprising, therefore, that they often file it without reading it, place it in a pile for future reading, or throw it away. Our sales literature must be a working tool, not just a future landfill.

Sales literature should become "working sales tools." Here's how:

Identify select areas in which the prospect expressed an interest.

- Highlight the specific bullet points or sentences supporting the prospect's areas of interest.
- Put a sticky note on the page so the free end becomes a tab above the rest of the pages.

What would happen if you got a brochure with a tab sticking out the top? Sure, you'd flip it open to that page.

What would you do if you saw a few phrases highlighted, particularly ones in which you are interested? You'd read them. And that's what the customer will do too.

Next time you send literature prepared in this manner, and you call the customer to follow up, be prepared to move forward because you won't be getting the old stall, "...Got your material but haven't had time to look at it."

But, if you sell certain products where emphasizing benefits is illegal (some pharmaceuticals) or otherwise frowned upon, then, of course, follow the guides of your industry.

A Psychological Truth

"If you sincerely try to understand another person's point of view first, then he or she becomes psychologically obligated to try to understand yours."

People with problems will continue to talk until they feel that you have clearly understood them and the situation, they find themselves in. The more they think you understand, the more weight they will give your recommendations.

If you try to present solutions before the customer believes you understand the situation, your credibility will be too low to make a positive impact. Even if your solution is correct, you cannot present it with sufficient credibility until you demonstrate how you've attempted to understand their situation.

This understanding can only come through the use of Active Listening Skills. More coming up in the next chapter. For now though, here is a quick overview of Active Listening Skills:

- **Acceptance Response:** Okay, yes, I see.
- **Repeating:** Repeat verbatim a keyword or phrase.
- **Paraphrasing:** Re-state it in your own words.
- **Reflecting:** Let the customer know which emotions you are seeing.
- **Clarifying:** Ask questions to move from generalizations to specifics.
- **Summarizing:** Paraphrase in summary form two or more topics or steps.

Blockers / Counter Blockers

Think about experiences you've had where it became clear that the person you were dealing with was not on the same page as you. What happened to any sense of rapport?

It doesn't take much to block rapport. Let's look at a few examples of rapport blockers and counter-blockers.

Blocker — — — — — — — — — — — — — — **Counter-Blocker**

Doubt You Know .... Understand First

Indifference .... Caring

Blaming & Criticizing .... Objective Fact-Finding

Superior Attitude .... Mutual Problem-Solving

Forget about it .... Follow up

The customer will doubt you know how to help until you earn the right to be heard. You do this by using your Active Listening Skills to understand them first. Recall our previous discussion about the Psychological Truth established by listening.

68% of customers said they moved to a competitor because they felt an attitude of indifference. For example, "It's too late in the day to get your order processed. You'll have to call back in the morning."

You can demonstrate your care by being sincere, genuine, and accepting during customer interactions. "Let me take down the information, and I'll get it processed first thing tomorrow morning when the staff arrives."

It's easy to blame and criticize. But that's also counterproductive to achieving your goal of helping customers. For example, "Obviously, you're just not experienced and qualified enough to figure out this quote. Some people just can't cut it."

Objective fact-finding counters this tendency. We know how to solve customers' problems, and that can sometimes come off as a superior attitude when none really exists. Focusing on using a step-by-step problem-solving model works better. For example, "Let's first separate the issues so we can look at them one at a time."

What kind of thoughts do you usually get when the customer service person says; I'll call you to let you know when it's ready? We've all had those experiences. So, if you want to keep the trust and rapport, you've worked so hard to establish, and then do what you say you'll do or don't say you'll do it.

Summary

To "trust" is to believe without proof. "Rapport" means to be in harmony with the other person. The greater the harmony in dress, speech, language, mannerisms, and so on, the more you feel you are like the other person, and the more you think you can predict how the person will act in certain situations. The more they are like you, the more you believe they would behave as you would. For example, you would expect someone who is a business person to arrive at a business meeting in business attire. Therefore, establishing rapport supports the creation of trust.

Job Aid - Trust & Rapport Building

COMMON GROUND

- Anything you share in common
- General (sunny weather)
- Business-oriented (bright outlook)
- Quality and Effective Products/Services

PACING & LEADING

- Mirror and match
- Pace them first and then take the lead

CREDENTIALS

- Defines your area of expertise and authority
- Appearance and behavior

BROCHURES / WEB

- Reflect on you, your company, your products/services
- Treat with respect

A PSYCHOLOGICAL TRUTH

- Sincerely try to understand the other person's point of view first so they will feel obligated to try to understand yours

5

Active Listening Skills for Business

Prevent errors and earn the right to be heard

Objectives

Many misunderstandings leading to costly errors, arguments, and lost productivity occurs because the person getting information to provide input, do a task, or problem-solve, did not "actively listen."

Sometimes we think we know the answer before the other person completes the thought. When we get ahead of ourselves, we can miss some small but essential piece of information that could change everything. Our mental processes automatically fill in the missing part with what we "think" should be there, and that's when the problems begin.

Knowing how to listen actively is a proven way to improve relationships with both internal and external customers.

After completing this chapter, you will know how to:

- Use acceptance responses
- Ask clarifying questions

- Repeat keywords, phrases, and numbers
- Paraphrase content
- Reflect emotions
- Summarize information
- Earn the right to be heard
- Use transition sentences

Introduction

To better understand the concept of "active listening," let's differentiate it from "passive listening."

Passive Listening is used when no feedback response is intended or needed, such as when listening to the radio or watching television.

Active Listening is used to actively provide verbal and nonverbal feedback to the speaker about your understanding of what is being communicated. The real trick is to do this without adding content to the conversation.

When you provide the speaker with an accurate interpretation of what s/he said, the more likely s/he is to feel that you genuinely understand their remarks.

A "Psychological Truth" states, "*...when we sincerely try to understand another person's point of view first, then they become psychologically obligated to try to understand ours.*"

This means that if you appear to have trouble getting someone to listen and to understand what you're trying to say, then the first strategy is to be the person who earns the right to be heard by being the first to listen. Using active listening skills is the way to make that happen.

Let's take a closer look at each of these skills.

Active Listening Skills

The secret to using Active Listening skills is to emphasize the listening part. That means being a sounding board. Not adding anything to the conversation, but viewing yourself as a mirror. Once the speaker acknowledges that you truly do understand, then and only then can you contribute new information and create a two-way communication.

Acceptance Responses

Using an acceptance response is inserting simple verbal utterances or words into the conversation.

For example, *"Yes," "I see," "Uh huh," "Okay," "Go on," "Tell me more,"* and so on.

Non-verbal communication can also be used. This could be as simple as nodding your head up and down to signify, "yes, I'm listening." This provides the feedback the speaker needs and does so without interrupting their flow of thought and speech."

Ask Clarifying Questions

Clarifying questions are used to better understand the speaker's situation better and move the conversation from broad generalizations to specific facts.

Let's look at an example conversation between a customer and a customer service representative (CSR):

- Customer: *"I sent the check weeks ago, and I got a statement that doesn't show my account has been credited."*
- CSR: *"That can be confusing; let me get a little more information. "How many weeks ago?"* (Clarifying question)
- Customer: *"I think it might have been two weeks."*

- CSR: *"Do you have the date of the current statement?"* (Clarifying question)
- Customer: *"Yes, I have it right here, and the date is _____."*
- CSR: *"Thank you."*

This exchange would naturally continue. The point here is to demonstrate the use of "clarifying questions. Let's continue now to the next Active Listening Skill known as "repeating."

Repeating

The purpose of repeating is to highlight keywords or phrases that indicate you have identified the most critical or complex components of the message.

Simply select the most important parts or those that might be easily misunderstood, and repeat them back to the speaker. Frequent misunderstandings occur with number sequences, addresses, words with double meanings ("here" and "hear"), and specific step-by-step instructions.

For example, if the customer says, *"The phone number where you can reach me during the day is 281-367-5599."*

You could reply with:

- a tone of understanding: *"281-367-5599."*
- a tone of expectation for additional information, *"5599?"*
- a question with a surprise inflection: *"5599? That's the same number as our customer service direct line."*

When something is confusing, or you want to make sure you heard it correctly. You can simply repeat what the person said back to them and get confirmation or correction. This is especially important for numbers and for spelling unusual words or names.

Paraphrase Content

Paraphrasing is restating, in your own words, your understanding of what you heard.

It is one of the more critical listening skills as it communicates understanding from your perspective.

The speaker needs this feedback to ensure what was intended to be communicated was indeed communicated.

Let's use the earlier situation to demonstrate a different way of providing speaker feedback.

Customer: *"I sent the check in two weeks ago, and today I got a statement, and it doesn't show my account had been credited."*

CSR: *"So, you sent the check in two weeks ago, and today, you got a statement that does not reflect your payment was made."* (Paraphrase)

Or, *"You sent in your check already, but it is not showing up on your account."* (Paraphrase)

Use paraphrasing when you want the speaker to know you understand what was said.

Reflect Emotion

Many conversations contain little if any, emotion. But for those that do, giving recognition to the emotion is an essential component of the communication that should not be ignored.

The old saying, "it's not what they said but how they said it," clearly applies whenever you hear emotional sounds in a person's voice.

To let the speaker know that you are aware of the associated emotions, you need to mention them in your feedback. You do this by naming the emotion or otherwise expressing the same emotion in your voice and mannerisms.

To effectively communicate emotions, you should be non-judgmental, sincere, genuine, and understanding.

CAUTIONS:

- Sympathy includes an element of sadness or pity. Few people want pity; they want to be understood.
- Empathy means understanding what they're feeling. For some, this means they have to feel what the other person is feeling, which, unfortunately, can quickly lead to burnout.
- Understanding is what they want from you, which means acknowledging their feelings and understanding their right to their feelings without feeling them yourself.

For all people, recognizing their emotions by naming them or otherwise indicating through voice tone or behavior that you understand they are experiencing them is an obviously important part of communication. This is true for both positive and negative emotions.

The intensity of emotions, especially negative ones, usually increases until they are recognized. If ignored, they could become too strong to deal with calmly.

Never underestimate the strength of an emotion. For example, don't ever say, "Oh, it's not that bad." Or, "it's not that big a deal." Or, "it's not that important." These words and sentiments will only increase the intensity of the emotion.

It is better to err toward a stronger emotion than a weaker one for both negative and positive feelings.

Some examples of phrases reflecting emotions:

A positive tone: *"That sounds like fun."* *"That's really exciting news."* *"How great is that?"*

A negative tone: *"I'm sorry to hear this is happening."* *"That's frustrating."* *"That's not right."*

Imagine talking with a customer in these situations:

Customer: *"I just got a letter from your company that says I have enough reward points to get the digital camera."*

CSR: (smile): *"That's really exciting news."*

To make this work effectively, you would:

- respond with a smile on your face to bring out your authentic voice tones
- genuinely feel happy for them

Customer: *"I'm having trouble finding this on your website."*

CSR: *"That can be frustrating, and I'm sorry you're experiencing that."*

To make this work effectively, you would:

- respond with a genuine sense of concern for them
- be sincere in your reflection
- hold unconditional positive regard for them

Summarize

Summarizing the conversation assures both the listener and speaker that a complex message was received and understood.

Summarizing uses all the other active listening skills. The difference between paraphrasing and summarizing is that you paraphrase one topic and summarize multiple topics.

Summarizing uses exact words and phrases where needed and paraphrasing content when a greater depth of understanding is important.

Summarizing could include restating clarifying questions as well as quoting acceptance responses.

Summarizing the entire conversation assures both the listener and speaker that the complete message was received and understood.

Let's review a customer situation and a couple of possible summarization responses.

Customer: *"I sent the check two weeks ago on the 25th, and today I got a statement which doesn't show my account has been credited. When I tried to make another purchase, I was notified that I was over the limit. That's never happened before!"*

Example summaries:

CSR: *Okay, let's pull all of this together. Your check was sent in on the 25th of the month, and you just received a statement that doesn't reflect your payment.*

"...Then, when you tried to make another purchase, you were over the limit. Thankfully, this hasn't happened before.

"...So, we need a clear this up and adjust your limit so that this won't happen again. Does that about sum up where we are now?"

Most of us already know these listening feedback skills. But what many of us don't do as well as we could, is to use them when necessary to ensure the right work gets done right, and use them to prevent misunderstandings.

The more comfortable we become using them here, the more likely it will be that we will use them when they are needed.

Tip: Practice with family, friends, co-workers, and customers.

A "Psychological Truth"

People are often unwilling to hear what you have to say in response to their situation until you acknowledge that you understand what they said. This builds your credibility by demonstrating you understand what they are trying to communicate. You might not be able to understand their experience if you've never had it, but you can understand what they are trying to communicate.

"When you sincerely try to understand another person's point of view (not necessarily agree with it), then they become psychologically obligated to try to understand your point of view."

You create this psychological truth by using active listening skills to ensure that what you heard is what they intended to communicate.

To develop this psychological truth:

- Listen carefully and completely
- Engage the active listening skills to confirm what you heard
- Get feedback from the speaker that your understanding of what you heard

is correct

Once you complete the above steps, you can:

- Make recommendations that will be heard
- Express your point of view
- Begin mutual problem-solving

Transition Sentences

Before you introduce information that does not agree with the other person, you must use a "Transition Sentence" or risk starting an argument.

Everyone knows that people are resistant to changing their minds. But, most people are willing to "make new decisions based on "new information" as long as they have a way to justify their previous point of view.

Transition Sentences:

- Provide support for the person's point of view without necessarily agreeing with it
- Provide a clear transition to a different point of view
- Help them save face - give them a way out if needed
- Refocus the person on participating in problem-solving

There are two parts to a transition sentence:

- A statement that supports the current view (without agreeing)
- An announcement that new information is coming

Examples of transition sentences:

- *"That's what I said when I first heard about this; then I found out..."*
- *"Ordinarily, that would be my conclusion too. However, when you consider..."*

- *"Based on what happened to you, I can certainly understand how you formed that opinion. I can also see that we did not communicate very clearly how that process works, so let me..."*
- *"That's a good point, and I'm glad you brought it up. When I first looked at this information, I came to the same conclusion, and then I found out..."*
- *"That's an important point I want to be sure to cover..."*
- *"Based on your application, that makes a strong point, so to compensate, we..."*
- *"Several of my customers came to the same conclusion until they found out..."*
- *"That makes sense, and it also makes sense when you add..."*

And the venerable often cited globally accepted transition sentence: *"I can understand how you could feel that way. In fact, several of my customers felt that way until they found out..."*

Remember that a transition sentence supports the person's point of view without necessarily agreeing with it. At the same time, it makes them receptive to a different point of view.

Try a quick practice using the transition sentence to deal with these statements.

Read the following customer statements, paraphrase your understanding, and then select one of the above transition sentences that best fit the situation. Of course, you can combine them or create new ones:

- *"Your company seems to be operating in the dark ages."*
- *"I don't think this is working for me. Maybe we better just cancel the service."*
- *"Your prices are way out of line."*

When different points of view exist, you will most likely have an argument on your hands without active listening skills and transition sentences.

If the person you're talking with thinks you don't understand their situation, how could they agree with what you're saying, especially if it's different from what they believe?

When and When Not to Use Active Listening Skills

Most of us already know these listening feedback skills. But what many of us don't do as well as we could, is to use them when necessary to ensure the right work gets done right and use them to prevent misunderstandings.

Be sure to use active listening skills when you:

- are engaged in a serious conversation
- will be asked to take action
- are in a problem-solving situation
- want to provide input, or you will be asked for input

Do not use active listening skills when a simple fact is all that is required. This is called a "fact response."

- *What time is it?*
- *How many more miles until we're there?*
- *Which direction do we go from here?*

Summary

Let's quickly review what you learned and what was reinforced in this book.

- Use acceptance responses to let the speaker know you're listening without interrupting their flow of thought.
- Ask clarifying questions to clear up any points that might be misinterpreted.
- Repeat keywords or phrases such as telephone, credit card, or purchase order numbers.

- Restate in your own words your understanding of what you heard.
- Identify and reflect emotions expressed to communicate that we understand the underlying message, such as a sense of urgency or seriousness.
- Summarize the entire communication by paraphrasing, reflecting, and repeating all the critical components of what the speaker said and then getting confirmation
- Use active listening skills collectively to establish your right to be heard.
- Use transition sentences to:
- Provide support for the person's point of view without necessarily agreeing with it
- Provide a clear transition to a different point of view
- Help them save face - give them a way out if needed
- Refocus the person on participating in problem-solving

For the most part, you already knew these skills. However, using them intentionally to confirm understanding, minimize communications errors, and earn the right to be heard are goals that can be easily obtained with these skills. Remember, the trick to using these skills to achieve these goals is to do so by adding as little new content to the conversation as possible.

Preventing arguments can be accomplished by introducing different points of view with a transition sentence. No one likes to be made wrong. This is a powerful way to communicate support.

Job Aid - Active Listening

1. Acceptance Responses: Verbal sounds, phrases (uh huh, yes, okay)
2. Ask Clarifying Questions: Request additional information to clarify
3. Repeat: Verbatim copy of the speaker's words or phrases
4. Paraphrase Content: Restate in your own words
5. Reflect Emotion: Recognize the emotion as it impacts the meaning of the communication
6. Summarize: Combine the key elements of the conversation – repeat,

paraphrase and reflect as indicated

6

Problem-Solving Model

Systematically solve difficult problems without creating new ones

Objectives

The costs associated with not having a systematic problem-solving model can be phenomenal. Usually, these costs get blamed on "bad" judgment or poor decision-making ability. But, in most cases, our research shows the underlying cause is not having or using a clearly defined systematic problem-solving process.

You might not know self-esteem is directly related to confidence in problem-solving abilities. The more different types of problems you gain experience in solving successfully, the higher and stronger your self-esteem becomes.

Confidence is built by repetitive successes with a process in a broad range of situations. A clearly defined problem-solving process will help you and your customers successfully and consistently meet the challenges you and your customers face.

This chapter will provide you with the knowledge to:

- Recognize the hazards associated with not using a systematic problem-solving process
- Use the steps of a systematic problem-solving process

Hazards of NOT Having a Problem-Solving Process

We all experience solving problems with varying degrees of success. Using a systematic method to solve problems can help avoid some of the more common hazards at the first sign of a problem.

Common hazards include:

- Jumping to conclusions
- Not getting enough of the correct information
- Attempting to solve problems that are beyond our control
- Solving one problem and creating another

Let's take a quick look at how these hazards impact your problem-solving ability and how a systematic problem-solving process can help prevent them.

Hazard 1: Jumping to Conclusions

When we receive information, we constantly process it to draw conclusions that help us order and make sense of it. Each piece of information creates a different picture in our heads, triggering other emotions.

Imagine that you have an important presentation tomorrow. A key component of your presentation has not arrived. You ordered weeks ago, followed up many times, and were assured it would arrive on time. And now you get a call from the store about your order. Read each line and then check to see what you're feeling.

- *I'm calling about your order*

- *We've had some problems*
- *Our supplier was out of stock*
- *But we managed to find a set at another store*
- *in Italy*
- *They agreed to ship it to us*
- *But it got held up in customs*
- *For about an hour*
- *Because the package was crushed*
- *But the inside container was not damaged*
- *It arrived today*
- *Now, after all that, the problem we have is*
- *We don't know how you want us to re-package it before we bring it out to you this afternoon.*

The emotional "roller coaster effect" occurs whenever we get a series of "good news" and "bad news" bits of information and jump to a conclusion about each one. You can imagine the impact this would have on your problem-solving ability.

Hazard 2: Not getting enough of the correct information

If we jump to conclusions and act without enough of the correct information, the results we get may not be what we have in mind and what the customer has intended. This is where we need to use the "who, what, where, when, how, and why" question series.

To make informed decisions, we first have to know the choices and what additional information we need to make the proper selection.

Imagine you received an e-mail with the following message, without a prior discussion or clarification about "it": "SEND IT TOMORROW."

What are some of the additional pieces of information you would need to complete that request? Trying to solve problems without enough of the right information can only lead to lots of guessing and many headaches.

Hazard 3: Attempting to solve problems that are beyond our control

We have been empowered to solve some problems. Some problems are beyond our abilities or authority. Still, others are simply insolvable with the resources available. Some issues cannot be corrected but perhaps might be prevented in the future.

People need to understand the limits of their problem-solving authority and recognize the problems that they are not going to be able to solve.

For example, we cannot control the rain, but we can make alternative plans to hold an event indoors in case of bad weather.

We cannot change a policy set at the highest levels in the company. Still, we can make sure that our supervisor is aware of the hardships it is causing so that they can communicate this information to the management.

When we're faced with unusual challenges, we need to make some decisions, including:

- Deciding if this is a problem that we can solve. Is it within our responsibility and authority?
- Deciding if it's solvable or not. If not, what are the options?
- Deciding if it's solvable now or in the future.

Hazard 4: Solving one problem and creating another

Any time action is required that is not in the normal course of doing things, we often create another challenge. This is simply because, in business, we are set up for a "standard operating procedure." Any exception to this procedure may cause someone to change an action later down the road. This can create additional challenges.

For example, if we put a "rush" on one order, will that cause other orders, already on the verge of being late, to truly be late? In which case will that cause all of the late orders to have the "rush" label applied to them?

While you're expediting one order, what's happening to the orders now hitting your desk? Are they backing up?

Check both upstream and downstream in your process before committing yourself to action. Verifying the availability of a solution before you promise can go a long way to easing tensions for you, the customer, and your company.

Self-Esteem

Self-esteem is also directly related to your confidence in your abilities to solve problems the world throws at you. Confidence is built by experiencing repeated successes in solving problems in a broad range of situations. Having a clearly defined problem-solving model will help you successfully and consistently resolve issues for yourself and your customers in a mutually satisfactory manner.

The more frequently you successfully use your problem-solving skills with a broad range of problems, the higher your esteem will be. But, take care. When you solve someone else s problem, rightfully theirs, your self-esteem is strengthened but diminishes theirs. Think about people who report to you, close friends, children, and others who seek you out. Be clear on whose problem needs to be solved. Your role may not be to solve the problem for them but rather to guide them through the problem-solving process with questions.

Problem-Solving Process Model

We need to recognize that while we all have our problem-solving styles, without a clearly defined process we all use, we cannot measure our effectiveness. Nor are we able to engage in process improvement.

Now consider the customer. If a solution doesn't work the way we think it should, we don't have a systematic way to analyze what went wrong and what we could do to fix it. Most of the time, we have to start over, and that is not an efficient way to meet our objectives, nor is it satisfying for the customer.

A clearly defined problem-solving process will help you systematically meet the challenges you and your customers face successfully and consistently.

Steps in an effective Problem-Solving Process:

1. Separate the Issues
2. Analyze "Presenting" Problem
3. Set Solution Objective
4. Define Criteria
5. Identify Optional Solutions
6. Select the Best Solution
7. Plan & Implement

Notice how some of the steps influence each other and note that if the solution isn't providing the desired results, you can always go back to the beginning to review and revise.

Since this problem-solving process model may be unfamiliar, there will be a listing of the steps at the beginning of each step discussion. Let's review each of these steps in greater detail.

Step 1. Problem-Solving Process

1. **Separate the Issues**
2. Analyze "Presenting" Problem
3. Set Solution Objective
4. Define Criteria
5. Identify Optional Solutions
6. Select the Best Solution
7. Plan & Implement

It is not uncommon for customers to present more than one problem at a time. Some may be the responsibility and authority of another department, others may require the involvement of other people, and still, others can be handled swiftly.

Always begin problem-solving by actively listening to the customer so that you get the necessary information to define the presenting problem. Then, the customer will be willing and able to hear solutions.

Review the following paragraph, identify, and identify each of the issues.

"This is Ann Harris down at Foster Inc., and we ordered a part from you that was supposed to be delivered today. It didn't show up, and I've got a service guy scheduled for tomorrow to install it. Plus, you double charged my credit card for the part. So, we need to get this taken care of now."

Separating the issues allows us to:

- Set priorities; determine which are yours to solve and which are someone else's responsibilities.
- Be prepared to help your customer enhance their self-esteem by engaging them in problem-solving. Doing this will improve trust and rapport and dramatically strengthen your relationship.

Usually, this first step and the next are done simultaneously so you can make better decisions on how to proceed.

Step 2. Problem-Solving Process

1. Separate the Issues
2. **Analyze the Presenting Problem**
3. Set solution objective
4. Define criteria
5. Identify optional solutions
6. Select the best solution
7. Plan and implement

The "Presenting Problem" is the problem the customer presents to us. It is a term that defines the immediate reason the customer contacted you.

These presenting problems are often symptoms of another more fundamental problem. For example, "The order is late" is a symptom caused by not having it in stock.

You could identify an entire series of causes that produce the symptom. This is the "domino effect."

For example, the order is late

- Because it was not in stock.
- Because we had a big sale and sold out.
- Because we didn't get our reorder in soon enough.
- Because manufacturing output was reduced.
- Because a significant piece of equipment failed.
- Because _____?

Treating the symptoms may be sufficient in many cases, but when the underlying problems continue aggravating customers, it is best to work on solving them.

To solve problems, you will need additional information. The questions to continually ask include:

- What is causing the problem the customer is presenting to you?
- Which symptoms or problems can I assist the customer with, and which are out of my control?

The process becomes:

- Define the symptoms of the presenting problem
- Identify the underlying causes of the presenting problem
- Classify causes as:
- Immediately solvable
- Solvable at a later time
- Solvable by someone else
- Not solvable
- Investigate to determine the actual cause as needed

Step 3. Problem-Solving Process

1. Separate the Issues
2. Analyze "Presenting" Problem
3. **Set the Solution Objective**
4. Define criteria
5. Identify optional solutions
6. Select the best solution
7. Plan and implement

The solution objective is what the customer wants when solving the present-ing problem.

If the presenting problem could recur, and the underlying cause is something an internal action could prevent, then the appropriate action items should be identified and implemented.

The objective is determined by answering the questions:

- "What does the customer want me to do?"
- "What is the outcome the customer wants to achieve?"
- "How can I define the presenting problem so we can work toward a solution that will satisfy the customer and prevent it from happening again?"

For example, if the customer didn't receive what they ordered, one solution objective would be to deliver what they ordered. Simple. Another objective could be to refund their money. Or another objective could be something they could use while the "back-ordered" product is available. Many options exist. You must ask and confirm what and when you think the customer wants.

Be aware of your corporate policy. It can influence how the customer's objective is achieved, if at all. However, for problem-solving, the first consideration is setting the solution objective based on what the customer is interested in achieving. This is then clarified with your active listening skills (see a review of Active Listening Skills later in this book) and guided by your capabilities and constraints.

Step 4. Problem-Solving Process

1. Separate the issues
2. Analyze the "presenting" problem
3. Set the solution objective
4. **Define criteria**
5. Identify optional solutions
6. Select the best solution

7. Plan and implement

When determining the criteria for a successful solution, we must both try to meet the customer's "solution objective" while at the same time making good business sense for us. In this way, we will achieve a win/win solution.

Criteria for a successful solution will take into account:

- "What are the customer's expectations?"
- "What are the customer's requirements?"
- "Do you have the capabilities to meet the requirements?"
- "What are the constraints within which you must operate?"

For example, if the customer has not received their order and the agreed "solution objective" is to get the merchandise to her by the end of the week. Then, the customer's criterion includes shipping the merchandise by the end of the week.

If your company can meet these expectations, then do so. However, if you have the constraint of only using two-day shipping for the fastest means that makes financial sense, then you will have to make that constraint known to the customer without causing any more upset.

The challenge you face when you tell a customer that you "can't" do something is that you are telling them they are about to experience a loss. When that happens, the grief process is automatically engaged, and the second stage is anger (see the discussion about anger in the next few pages for more information). To prevent triggering anger, always remember that when you **tell a customer about something you can't do, be sure to follow along with the word "but" (to erase the "can't" part of the statement) and then tell them what you "can do."**

The word "but" erases the unpleasant and anger-producing sting of the word "can't." For example, "You're doing a good job, but..." See how the words "You're doing a good job" were literally erased from consideration as a real sentiment in your mind?

Following up with what you can do puts the process back on track. Remember, you can always do something, even if it's just noting the customer's concern to your supervisor.

Step 5. Problem-Solving Process

1. Separate the Issues
2. Analyze "Presenting" Problem
3. Set Solution Objective
4. Define Criteria
5. **Identify Optional Solutions**
6. Select the Best Solution
7. Plan & Implement

Very often, there are alternate solutions that will satisfy the criteria. For example, you could offer to refund money, send a substitute product, credit the account, expedite the order, locate another product, and so on. Modify the objective, criteria, and solutions until optional workable solutions are developed.

The Brainstorming Process: Brainstorming is a valuable method of developing options.

Phase One: Generate as many ideas as possible. This simple process can be done with the customer, colleagues, supervisor, or yourself. The objective is to generate a large or realistic quantity of ideas. The critical quality of the ideas is never questioned during the idea-generating phase.

Phase Two: Begin to apply the criteria to the ideas to select a solution to the problem. This begins to refine the ideas and narrow the total number of options to a manageable number. Prioritize the solution list.

Phase Three: Identify realistic options that meet the criteria and can be presented to and discussed with the customer.

Step 6. Problem-Solving Process

1. Separate the Issues
2. Analyze "Presenting" Problem
3. Set Solution Objective
4. Define Criteria
5. Identify Optional Solutions
6. **Select the Best Solution**
7. Plan & Implement

Discuss the agreed-upon criteria with the customer before the optional solutions are presented. When you offer the options, summarize how each solution meets the requirements.

Anticipate obstacles and minimize risk by selecting and presenting only those solutions in which you have the most control over the outcome.

Cost-Benefit Analysis: Solutions can quickly get expensive. Chartering a jet to hand-deliver a $500 order would not be the most cost-efficient way to solve the customer's problem of not receiving an order. A $35.00 "hotshot" courier charge may be a better solution.

The questions that must be continually asked include:

- What will it cost the customer and (potentially our company) if the problem is not solved?

· Is there a mutually agreeable solution that will solve most of the problem, thereby minimizing most of the costs?

Any final solution selected must be a win/win for both the company and the customer. Any other option (lose/win, win/lose, and lose/lose) is unacceptable. The cost of the solution should not exceed the value to be gained.

Presenting the selected solution:

Tell how each one will meet the customer's criteria.

"We can ship by one of two regular overnight carriers. The arrival is not as early but should still be there shortly after the start of the business day. Or, we could use an overnight trucking service since the distance is not over 300 miles, which would normally deliver at 8:00 am, but this is not a guaranteed service. A third option is to ship a partial shipment out express with the remainder going by normal ground delivery."

State your recommendation positively.

"Using partial shipment is probably the most cost-effective way of meeting all your requirements."

Let the customer make the final decision.
   "Which would you prefer?"

Step 7. Problem-Solving Process

1. Separate the Issues
2. Analyze "Presenting" Problem
3. Set Solution Objective
4. Define Criteria

5. Identify Optional Solutions
6. Select the Best Solution
7. **Plan & Implement**

Suggest ways to the customer how to implement the selected solution.

Divide the implementation of the solution into sequential steps. Outline what all parties involved must do and when it must be done to achieve the desired results.

Ask for feedback from the customer to ensure that they understand any action items they have for implementing the solution.

If the solution does not solve the entire problem or does not resolve all the customer's concerns, then tell the customer what is and what is not included.

Ask the customer to accept that you are solving all that you can, given the limits of your authority or capability. This will help to reassure the customer and gain their understanding that you are doing the best job possible.

To plan and implement the best solution:

- Restate the solution objective
- Define the solution in steps
- Identify who will take what actions
- Determine when they will be done
- Explain how you will know they have been done
- Identify and locate any resources needed that are not immediately at your disposal

Supporting Skills – Review Active Listening and Defusing Anger

Active Listening Skills – Quick Review

Always begin problem-solving by actively listening to the customer so that you get the necessary information to separate the issues and define the presenting problem. Secondly, use your active listening skills (reflect emotions) to release any negative emotions so that you can work more effectively with the customer to solve the problem.

You earn your right to be heard by establishing a **"Psychological Truth,"** which states, *"If you sincerely try to understand another person's point of view first, then he/she becomes psychologically obligated to try to understand yours."*

Once someone knows that you truly understand their issues, you have established your right to be heard and bolstered your standing to participate in a problem-solving session. You achieved this by using your active listening skills. Let's take a quick review of these skills:

- **Acceptance Responding** – "Okay, Yes, I see."
- **Repeating** - Repeat verbatim a keyword or phrase
- **Paraphrasing content** - Restate it in your own words
- **Reflecting emotions** - Letting the customer know which emotions you are seeing (critical skill for defusing strong emotions)
- **Asking Clarifying Questions** - Ask questions to move from generalizations to specifics
- **Summarizing** - Paraphrase in summary form two or more topics or steps

Using these skills without adding content or opinion is the difficult part. Just mirroring their expressions will go a long way to building trust and rapport, establishing or reinforcing an empathetic supporting relationship, and earning your right to be heard.

By the simple act of actively listening to the person, you are demonstrating that you care. As you will see, this is the second step to defusing anger, and active listening builds the foundation for the effectiveness of the defusing anger steps.

Summary

The **Problem-Solving Process Model** taught here is one that enables an in-depth and systematic way to move toward solutions for simple to complex problems.

1. Separate the Issues
2. Analyze "Presenting" Problem
3. Set Solution Objective
4. Define Criteria
5. Identify Optional Solutions
6. Select the Best Solution
7. Plan & Implement

Steps for solving problems you're familiar with are often combined and re-sequenced to get to the desired solution. Once specific capabilities and constraints are known, you don't have to continually revisit that step unless the problem is more perplexing than meets the eye. In that case, careful attention to detail will most likely win the day.

Two supportive interpersonal communication skill-sets enhance your ability to work with others in helping them clarify the problems and move past strong emotions that might inhibit their ability to come to a successful resolution. These skill sets are active listening and defusing anger.

It makes sense to listen to the customer to understand the problem they're facing. Doing so also earns you the power of "psychological truth, " which motivates people to want to hear what you say.

Problems sometimes come with the heavy weight of negative emotions, which often cloud the issue, making using clear and rational problem-solving complex, if not impossible. Therefore, releasing or defusing these emotions makes sense before serious efforts to engage the customer in the problem-solving process.

Job Aid - Problem-Solving

1. Separate the Issues
2. Analyze "Presenting" Problem
3. Set Solution Objective
4. Define Criteria for Successful Solution
5. Develop Optional Solutions
6. Select the Best Solution
7. Plan & Implement

- Steps 3 – 6 can be reworked as each one is developed.
- Results of Step 7 are matched to the resolution of the Presenting Problem (Step 2).

7

Defusing Customer Anger

Recognize Anger and Quickly Defuse It

Objectives

Sometimes, the customer senses that a problem could cause them to experience a loss. The threat of loss triggers the grief process, and anger is the third (sometimes second) stage. With an upset customer, if we solve the problem and do not first take care of the customer's emotions, we end up with a **satisfied angry customer**.

Angry customers will tell many other potential customers about the problem. Even though the problem was solved, they are still upset and often feel that it shouldn't have happened in the first place.

After completing this chapter, you will know how to:

- Define anger and its purpose
- List the three ways of expressing anger
- Describe the three things angry people want and the sequence in which they want them
- Use active listening skills to communicate understanding

- Use the active listening skill "reflecting emotion" to defuse the emotion
- Recognize phrases that can evoke anger and those phrases that can prevent anger

Section 1: Understand the Emotions of Anger

Definitions

Anger is an emotional response to any perceived threat that might result in real or imagined loss of something we have now or something we want to have.

The loss could be personal such as a loss of self-esteem, happiness, or embarrassment.

The loss could also be economical, material, environmental, or many other areas the person cares about and has a vested interest in protecting.

The purpose of anger is to provide the physical energy necessary to overcome or destroy this threat. When this emotion is triggered, energy-producing chemicals are pumped throughout the body, especially the large muscles.

The intensity of anger can range from mild annoyance to rage.

Loss

Whenever anger is present with any degree of intensity, a loss is also present, and loss is the common denominator. The loss can be real or imagined, past, present, or future.

Think about a time when you were angry. Don't dwell on the emotion itself; be objective about it. Can you identify the actual or potential loss that triggered that anger? Most likely, you can. If you look at other times when you were upset, you will always find that loss was present. If you are still angry about it, your anger has not been defused properly.

Section 2: Recognize Anger in Others - Expression

You now know that anger is a response to a loss, real or imagined. But not everyone expresses it the same way, making it more difficult for us to identify anger in others.

There are three ways in which people express their anger:

- **Aggressive:** anger expressed outwardly in an attacking manner
- **Passive:** anger expressed inwardly in a seething compliant manner
- **Assertive:** anger expressed directly and clearly in a firm way

We can recognize the style of expression by both the behavior exhibited by the angry person and the feelings that behavior evokes in us.

For the most part, people use all three expressions of anger. The circumstance and setting will determine how a person expresses anger. That means, under the right conditions, we can express anger passively, aggressively, and assertively.

Aggressive Expression

People who express their anger aggressively do so at great risk to themselves and those who become their target. Physical, mental, and emotional exhaustion will eventually take its toll. It is the aggressive expression of anger that causes most of us to want to avoid dealing with upset customers. Aggressive behavior is the easiest of the three expressions of anger to recognize.

Aggressive expressions of anger include:

- Standing up for rights
- Having little regard for the rights of others
- Threatening and blaming everyone else
- Appearing self-serving and self-righteous
- Prefer a win/lose situation because when they win, you must lose
- Being loud, dominating, and demanding, using menacing voice tones
- Becoming abusive
- Expressing anger outwardly
- Trying to make you angry too so you will understand (See how you like it!)

When someone expresses anger aggressively toward us, to some extent, we feel:

- Hurt
- Humiliated
- Fearful
- Defensive
- Revengeful
- Resentful
- Depreciated
- Distrustful

For example, you might hear someone expressing their displeasure aggressively using loud tones, red-faced and shaking their finger at you, saying, *"I've just about had it with you and your incompetence!"*

Passive Expression

People who express their anger passively have abandoned their rights and are not honest about what they feel or need. These customers may apologize unnecessarily and meekly do exactly as instructed. The customer's goal is to avoid confrontation or rejection and to be "likable."

Passive expressive customers are often mistaken for happy customers. We assume that everything is probably okay if they don't complain. They appear calm, logical, and accepting of whatever information they share.

If they become upset with what they perceive as "bad" service, they may not tell us but will tell many other people about it. Research shows that 96% of dissatisfied customers won't complain. These people often express their anger through passive compliance.

Examples of passive expressions of anger are:

- Withdrawal
- Not doing what you ask
- Minimal compliance
- Being late to order, attend meetings, and turn in reports
- Developing physiological complaints
- Becoming apologetic
- Abandoning their own rights to their feelings and their needs

When someone is expressing their anger passively, we feel:

- Guilt
- Pity
- Loss of respect
- Superiority
- Frustration
- Anger

Think about a time when you were dissatisfied with the service at a restaurant. The bright and cheery wait-staff person arrives and asks, *"How is everything?"* More often than not, we use passive expression and respond with *"Fine."* And after saying that, did you leave a customary size tip? *"Probably not."* We all use this expression under certain circumstances, don't we?

Assertive Expression

Customers who express anger assertively support their rights and express their opinions and feelings honestly. They do not violate the rights of other people. They articulate with diplomacy but in a concise manner.

Their words are well-chosen and to the point. You will know exactly what they expect and where you stand with them. They may be angry, but by expressing themselves assertively, they remained in control and focused on their goal. They negotiate honestly.

This expression of anger is outward but channeled through a mechanism that helps them maintain a healthy perspective and control. Assertive customers generally make demands and indicate their authority as soon as possible in the conversation.

They are generally very clear about their expectations and needs. They often appear to be all business, no play. They seem focused on the task at hand and unwilling to detour into elaborate social amenities.

Assertive expressions of anger:

- Making demands but using logic and control
- Taking charge of the conversation by insisting they be heard
- Being all business, no play
- Standing up for their rights but not violating the rights of others
- Respecting the needs of others
- Negotiating honestly and openly

What we feel when someone is expressing their anger assertively:

- Respected
- Valued

· Trusting

For example, you might hear someone expressing their displeasure assertively as *"This is not an acceptable situation. I'm concerned that we're nearing the deadline we promised would be met. That being the case, I think you'll agree that we'll need to -escalate the problem-solving to a higher level in the organization where they've got more options available."*

Physiological Effects of Anger

When strong positive or negative emotions are felt, some changes occur physiologically. These changes are apparent. There are also changes in the ability to access various parts of the brain needed for reasoning that is no longer available while the emotion remains in control.

For example, when a person is angry, you might recall these descriptions:

· **Red flushed** look caused by blood rushing to the face
· **Seeing red** caused by tiny blood vessels breaking inside the eye and the person is looking through red blood cells
· **Getting steamed** caused by increased blood flow increases body temperature
· **Hot under the collar** caused by increased blood flow around the shoulders and neck with a tie-on prevents heat from escaping, and the person is literally "hot under the collar."
· **Pain in the neck** caused by muscles getting stiff from tension

So, why you can't reason with an upset customer? The ability to reason is carried out in areas of the brain that are cut off by the overload of emotions flooding in. These emotions dominate and take over the neurological circuits needed to get the information to the parts of the brain used for reasoning.

The stronger the emotion, the less reasoning ability the person has in their control. Think about a "dimmer" switch on the lights in a room. The brightness of the lights represents intellectual reasoning ability. The brighter they are, the more reasoning power is available. However, the stronger the emotion becomes, the more the switch is turned in the direction that lowers the brightness of the lights.

So, until the emotions are calmed, the person will not be able to accept any reasonable solution you might offer. Not that they don't want to. They do. But with the emotions in play, they simply can't access the parts of the brain that enable them to think logically or rationally at this time.

Section 3: Skills Required to Defuse Anger

Defusing anger requires you to have a couple of common skills: active listening and problem-solving process skills.

Active Listening Skills – Quick Review

You earn your right to be heard by establishing a **"Psychological Truth,"** which states, *"If you sincerely try to understand another person's point of view first, then he/she becomes psychologically obligated to try to understand yours."*

Establishing this right to be heard is achieved using your active listening skills.

Let's now take a quick review of the active listening skills:

- **Acceptance Responses** (Okay, yes, I see)
- **Repeat** (Repeat verbatim a keyword or phrase)
- **Paraphrase content** (Restate it in your own words)
- **Reflect emotion** (Recognize the emotions being expressed)
- **Ask Clarifying Questions** (Move from generalizations to specifics)
- **Summarize** (Paraphrasing in summary form, two or more topics or steps)

Using these skills without adding content or opinion is the difficult part. Just mirroring their expressions will go a long way to building trust and rapport, establishing or reinforcing an empathetic supporting relationship, and earning your right to be heard.

The first step in Defusing Anger is your listening skill of "reflecting emotion." But even before you do this, you must engage the person and get them to tell you what's happening with them. When they direct their concerns (sometimes tirades) to you, then you are in a position to automatically establish your right to be heard ("Psychological Truth").

Working with upset customers is challenging. If you begin to feel their pain and become upset or defensive, you fall prey to being emotionally "empathetic." You now feel what they feel.

Once your emotions are in play, your effectiveness rapidly diminishes. Instead, just as the psychological truth states, they don't want your pity (sympathy). They don't want you to come unglued, feeling their pain (empathy). Instead, they just want to be "understood," which includes understanding their right to their feelings.

If you choose not to listen actively, the person who expresses their anger aggressively will continually intensify their efforts to try to get you upset, so you will finally "understand" how they feel. To effectively communicate emotions, you should be non-judgmental, sincere, genuine, and understanding.

By the simple act of actively listening to the person, you are demonstrating that you care. As you will see, this is the second step to defusing anger, and active listening builds the foundation for the effectiveness of these steps.

Problem-Solving Process – Quick Review

Working through a systematic problem-solving process will go a long way in helping the customer adjust to a new reality.

There are many different ways in which people solve problems. Your company may have a prescribed process for you to follow. Problem-solving abilities are not only a functional "life skill" applicable in all areas of your life; they are also prized skills for business. Here is a brief overview of a problem-solving process:

1. Separate the issues
2. Analyze the presenting problem
3. Determine the solution objective
4. Identify the criteria for a successful solution
5. Develop optional solutions that meet the criteria
6. Select the best solution
7. Plan and implement the best solution

A systematic problem-solving process that includes the customer will produce solutions acceptable to both the company and the customer.

Let's quickly review this problem-solving model.

1. **Separate the issues.** Customers often present more than one problem at a time. Work on solving those that are in your authority to solve. Prioritize solving those that by their relationship to other issues will also solve those.
2. **Analyze the presenting problem.** What problem is the customer bringing to you? Is this a problem you can solve or a symptom of another problem?
3. **Determine the solution objective.** Know what you're trying to achieve. Find out what the customer wants. It may be as simple as getting delivery

of a part they didn't receive. Or, it may be more complex, in that the customer wants to make sure that their company doesn't have a repeat performance of a problem that can be prevented and wants to meet to write up a procedure to prevent the problem.

4. **Identify the criteria for a successful solution.** Work within the customer's expectations and within your capabilities and constraints.

5. **Develop optional solutions that meet the criteria.** If the problem is out of the ordinary, try to develop at least three acceptable solutions through brainstorming. You can brainstorm with colleagues, supervisors, or customers based on your company's policy.

6. **Select the best solution.** All things being equal, let the customer select what will work best for them.

7. **Plan and implement the best solution.** Follow up on any solution you implement.

You can use the feedback from various steps to modify other steps to get a satisfactory outcome.

You already have a problem-solving model that you use continually to solve large and small challenges you face every day in all areas of your life. You often solve problems intuitively without needing deep analysis, which enables you to combine many steps. Other times, you take more time to dig into the details and look at the situation from different perspectives. When you dig deeper, you follow something similar to the steps defined here more closely.

Words and Phrases that Trigger Anger

You sometimes have to say "no" to a customer. Knowing how to say it that will make the difference between making them angry or making them an ally.

Some frequently used words and phrases can cause a person to sense that a loss may occur. These words and phrases could include:

- *"I can't."*
- *"I won't."*
- *"No."*
- *"Policy won't allow."*
- *"That's not my job."*
- *"Sorry"*
- *"Those are the rules."*
- *"You can't."*
- *"You must comply."*

Whenever you have to say "no" to a customer, always follow it with what you "can do." You " can always do something," even if it is to make a note in the record or pass it on to your supervisor.

Increase its power and effectiveness by using the word "but." The conjunction or connector "but" is an eraser. It erases everything that was said in front of it. For example, *"You're doing a great job, BUT!"* Here you've just erased everything in front of the word "but."

So, when you say something like, *"I can't* (do whatever), always follow that with, *"...but, what I can do is...."*

"I can't let you take that with you, but what I can do is ship the next one available to you."

"However," is also an eraser. It is less abrupt than "but." It is useful for those situations that require more sensitivity. For example, *"Our company policy is very specific, and I won't be able to do that. However, I will let my supervisor know about your situation, and maybe they will make some adjustments in the future."*

Phrases that follow this model include:

- *"But what we can do is..."*

- *"But, next time, it would help if..."*
- *"But I am..."*
- *"But would you..."*
- *"However, what needs to be done is..."*
- *"However, if you could place your order by ...."*

There are guidelines to help us communicate so we don't inadvertently trigger anger.

- Focus on what you and the customer CAN DO rather than can't do. You " can always do something," even if it is to make a note in the record or pass it on to your supervisor. If you catch yourself saying, "CAN'T...," use the connector "but" and follow it immediately by saying what you CAN DO.
- Focus on the ISSUE, not the person. Instead of saying, "you have to fill out the form, " say, "...the system needs the information from the form to make sure the order can be tracked." Or, "...the schedule is full those days. What I can do is put you on the waiting list and also make an appointment the following week to make sure you have a reserved time."
- "WILL DO" has power limitations. If you tell the customer that you will have someone, call them back, you will need to be able to make that person make the call physically. If not, say, "I'll 'ask' her to call you."

Section 4: Three Steps to Defuse Anger

Angry people suffer a sense of loss, real or imagined, past, present, or future. Loss evokes the grief process that involves a mixture of emotions and behaviors.

Angry people want three things:

1. They want to be understood.
2. They want to know someone cares.

3. They want to be helped in preventing (further) loss.

As soon as every good problem solver hears about a problem that needs solving, the focus becomes on solving the problem logically, without regard to human emotions. That's the nature of a problem solver. However, problem-solving, without first taking care of the person's emotions, will create a satisfied angry customer.

And for all the exceptionally adept problem solvers out there reading this, you should know that only after the person has released enough of their anger and has calmed down enough to regain access to their rational thinking capabilities can you dig in and problem-solve with great effectiveness.

How and why, it works: Follow the Grief Process

Several descriptions of grief processes relate to different researchers' perspectives. However, a constant seems to be two emotions (anger and sadness) and a state of being (objectivity).

1. **Anger** – Be understood – Step 1. Recognize: name the emotion to defuse it.
2. **Sadness** – Be cared about – Step 2. Apologize: no-fault for showing you care.
3. **Objectivity** - Prevent or reverse loss – Step 3. Solutionize: initiate problem-solving

Anger serves the function of generating significant amounts of physical and mental energy necessary to stop or reverse a loss. You see this in protests and riots in the streets, for example. Or people yelling at public officials or each other. Whenever you see a fight or a heated argument (different than a debate), you can be certain that Active Listening Skills were not used.

What is important here is that when you notice anger, you can let the person know you recognize it by calling it by name. Naming it shows you "understand" what they're feeling and, in turn, defuses it. When you sense the energy going out of anger, the person will most likely move into a state of sadness to eventually accept the reality of the situation.

Sadness serves the purpose of reintegrating the mind into a new reality. During this phase, the brain actually rewires itself by breaking some neuronal connections while making others. This is why this phase of grieving is so important, especially in the case of a severe loss.

At this phase, the person just wants to know and sense that someone cares about them and their feelings. They don't want pity; they don't want you to feel what they're feeling. Instead, they just want an understanding of their situation and them.

Now one practical way you could show you care is with a no-fault apology ("I'm sorry this happened to you" or, "I'm sorry for your loss") or some other method that expresses caring, as we'll soon discuss. When the grieving person becomes resolved to accept the reality of the situation, it's now time to move to problem-solving to attempt to stop, minimize, or reverse the loss.

For example, people entering the problem-solving phase often get involved in causes that will keep other people from having to go through what they did.

Let's review these steps in greater detail to learn optional ways each step can be done. We'll take it from the point where the person first shows anger.

Defusing Anger Step 1 – Recognize the Emotion [Recognize]

You can communicate your recognition of the emotion by calling it by name, along with matching the seriousness and intensity with your level of concern, body language, and tone of voice. This helps defuse emotion. Ignoring the emotion only causes it to intensify.

When the person is upset, you must find out what happened before you can help them. You can say, *"I can see you're really upset; tell me what's going on."*

You will continually use your active listening skills to show caring, continue to recognize their emotional state, and set up the transition to problem-solving.

Calling anger by name communicates that you do understand and begins the defusing process. Active Listening will provide the supporting power to "call it by name" and therefore allow it to have its greatest impact.

Sample "anger" words: Some words reflect the emotion of anger. While actively listening to the customer, simply call the emotion by name.

- agitated
- disturbed
- infuriated
- perturbed
- aggravated
- enraged
- irate
- provoked
- angry
- exasperated
- rattled
- annoyed
- irritated
- troubled
- bothered
- frustrated
- mad
- unnerved

- concerned
- furious
- miffed
- unsettled
- distressed
- incensed
- outraged
- upset

To give you a better idea about how this works, use any of the words in this in the sample sentence below to fill in the blanks.

- *"No wonder you're _____."*
- *"I understand how _____ you are about this situation."*
- *"This would cause anyone to be _____."*
- *"I know this would _____ me."*
- *"I get that you're very _____."*

Here are a few examples of communicating your understanding of their emotion:

- *"I can certainly understand how **upsetting** this can be."*
- *"No wonder you're **irritated**."*
- *"If it were me, I'd be **mad** as a hornet."*
- *"That's enough to make you **furious**...."*
- *"No wonder you're **unsettled**. If that happened to me, I'd be **rattled** too."*
- *"That's **annoying**, to say the least."*
- *"If this happened to me, I'd be **upset** too."*
- *"Based on what happened, no wonder you're **frustrated**."*
- *"That's just got to be so **infuriating**."*
- *"You've got just to be **screaming**."*
- *"This is very **disturbing** to me, as I'm sure it is to you."*
- *"That's so **aggravating**."*

Listening doesn't mean letting the person rant and rave for hours. Rather, it means getting essential information by asking clarifying questions (active listening skills). As soon as you know the score, you can call the emotion by name. You can quickly defuse the emotion by having the same intensity as they do.

Calling the emotion by name defuses it. Continuing through the next two steps helps the person finish the last two steps of the grief process. This is important to keep the anger defused.

For example, if the customer tells you by the tone of voice, body language, or directly that they are upset about a situation, the steps would then be:

Step 1 – *Recognize* the emotion: *"I can understand you're **upset** about this..."*

Step 2 – Show caring during the Sadness phase of Grief: *"....and I'm really sorry for the confusion this must be causing."* No fault apology. *Apologize.*

Step 3 – Initiate problem-solving during the Objectivity phase Grief: *"...let's see what we can do to clear it up."* *Solutionize.*

By recognizing their emotion, you will move them from the Anger phase of Grief into the Sadness phase.

Defusing Anger Step 2 – Show Caring [Apologize]

People who are sincere and genuine when they use their active listening skills are viewed as people who care.

The more you hold an unconditional positive regard attitude about other people and the more you have a propensity to treat people as begin worthy of respect rather than foes, the more they will perceive you as a caring human being.

You can also show you care about the feelings they are experiencing by reflecting that in your tone of voice and behavior. Shaking your head "no," making harrumphing sounds, or other similar vocalizations can make it clear you "understand" what they're feeling without feeling it yourself.

Another way to do this is to offer a **"no-fault" or "no blame" style apology** for the pain they are feeling. You're expressing that you are sorry the situation occurred to them. But it is also an apology that does not involve blame.

This method is simply to say that you are sorry they are having that type of experience. **You're expressing that you are sorry the situation occurred (to them or anyone).**

However, if it is a mistake you made, you can own up to it with a similar sincere apology. It's not so much apologizing for the error; rather, it's the upset feeling (anger) the person is feeling for which you would apologize.

For example, Step 2 below illustrates one way to give a "no-fault" apology and demonstrate that you really care for the trouble the person is experiencing.

Step 1 – Recognize the emotion during the Anger stage of the Grief Process: *"I can understand you're **upset** about this..."*

Step 2 – Show caring during the Sadness stage of the Grief Process: *"...and I'm really sorry for the confusion this must be causing."* No fault apology works well and is easy to remember to do with the mnemonic: *Recognize, Apologize, Solutionize.*

Step 3 – Initiate problem-solving during the Objectivity stage of the Grief Process: *"...let's see what we can do to clear it up."* (Solutionize)

Other ways to show caring:

- *"I'm really sorry you are having this experience."*
- *"No one should have to go through that."*
- *"And I'm really sorry that this happened to you."*
- *"It shouldn't have happened."*
- *"It seems we've made an error."*
- *"I apologize for the trouble this is causing."*
- *"I can't begin to tell how sorry I am about this."*
- *"Please know how badly we feel that this happened."*
- *"I'm sorry, this just isn't right."*
- *"You sound very concerned."*
- *"We're also very concerned that this could have happened."*
- *"I'm sorry. No one should have to go through that."*

Sounds and incomplete expressions also show caring:

- *"Oomph, that shouldn't have happened."*
- *"Ouch! What a mess that is."*
- The facial expression of concern, slowly shaking head from side to side (suggesting "no").

Once they recognize your caring, regardless of how you communicate it, you move them from the Sadness stage of the Grief Process into the Objectivity stage, where they are receptive to and capable of rational problem-solving.

Defusing Anger Step 3 – Problem-Solve to Prevent, Minimize, or Reverse Loss [Solutionize]

Now that the energy underlying the emotion of anger is being dissipated and sadness has resolved itself and re-energized itself into objectivity, the next step is to focus on the problem-solving process to prevent further or future loss. See step 3 below.

For example:

Defusing Anger Step 1 – Recognize the emotion during the Anger stage of the Grief Process: *"I can understand you're **upset** about this..."*

Defusing Anger Step 2 – Show caring during the Sadness stage of the Grief Process: *"....and I'm really sorry for the confusion this must be causing."*

Step 3 – Initiate problem-solving during the Objectivity stage of the Grief Process: *"...let's see what we can do to clear it up."*

Other ways to say, *"Let's work together to solve this problem."*

- *"Let's see what we can do to clear this up."*
- *"Let me get some additional information so I can dig deeper into how we can help fix the problem."*
- *"Let's look at the options we've got to fix this."*

Other ways to engage the problem-solving process might be:

- *"...Let's see what we have to work with here..."*
- *"...So, as I see it, there are really three issues to tackle..."*
- *"...The challenge we've got is that I can't get those parts to you today, but what I can do is..."*

Be aware that if you can and do solve the problem before defusing the anger, you will have an angry, satisfied customer. So, in all cases, you would be advised to reevaluate and defuse the anger by guiding the person through the grief process.

Summary

Anger is triggered when a person perceives an actual or imagined loss happening in the past, present, or future. Anger causes the body to respond chemically (re-energized, for example) to provide the energy needed to stop the loss. Anger can range in strength from mild annoyance to anger to rage.

Anger shows up naturally in the Grief Process, and the Grief Process is a normal response to mourning a loss.

Emotional events, usually fear (of loss) related, cause the amygdala to trigger the (usually) aggressive expression of anger.

Primary skills needed to defuse anger include Active Listening and Problem-Solving. The primary personal attitudes of unconditional positive regard, genuineness, and sincerity make using these skills a part of your being. This is readily communicated, sensed, and recognized by others, upset or not.

Words and phrases that suggest a "loss" will trigger anger. The guideline is that when you catch yourself saying, "CAN'T...," use the connector "but" and follow it immediately by saying what you CAN DO.

The three steps to defuse anger are:

1. **Recognize** the emotion during the Anger phase of Grief: *"I can under-stand you're upset about this..."*
2. **Apologize** (no fault) to show caring that they are going through this during the Sadness phase of Grief: *"...and I'm really sorry for the confusion this must be causing."*
3. **Solutionize** by initiating problem-solving during the Objectivity phase of Grief: *"...let's see what we can do to clear it up."*

Be aware that you may have to repeat these three steps several times, along with using your other active listening and problem-solving skills to defuse the emotion completely. This is especially true when the emotion is strong or has spread to several different areas in a person's life.

Job Aid – Defusing Anger

Step 1. <u>RECOGNIZE</u> AND REFLECT THE EMOTION
<u>How?</u> Expressions ❑ Aggressive ❑ Passive ❑ Assertive
Active Listening Skills
❑ Acceptance Responses ❑ Ask Clarifying Questions
❑ Repeat ❑ Paraphrase content ❑ Reflect Emotion
❑ Summarize

Step 2. SHOW CARING - <u>APOLOGIZE</u>
<u>How?</u> Actively listen with empathy, genuineness, and sincerity. Provide a "no-fault" apology for the negative experience and emotions. Treat them with respect and the positive regard of a friend, not a foe. Explain as needed but don't argue or defend.

Step 3. PROBLEM SOLVE - <u>SOLUTIONIZE</u>
<u>How?</u> Transition to the problem-solving process.
❑ Separate issues ❑ Analyze "Presenting Problem."
❑ Set Solution Objective ❑ Identify Criteria for Success ❑ Develop Optional Solutions
❑ Select Best Solution ❑ Plan, Implement and Follow up

Aggressive Expression

Behavior:

- Standing up for rights
- Having little regard for the rights of others
- Threatening and blaming everyone else
- Being self-serving and self-righteous
- Prefer a win/lose situation because when they win, you must lose.
- Being loud, dominating, and demanding, using menacing voice tones

- Becoming abusive
- Expressing anger outwardly
- Trying to make you angry, too, so you will understand

You Feel:

- Hurt
- Humiliated
- Fearful
- Defensive
- Revengeful
- Resentful
- Depreciated
- Distrustful

Passive Expression

Behavior:

- Abandoned their rights
- Not honest about what they feel or need
- Apologize
- Meek acceptance
- Withdraw
- Minimally compliant
- Avoid confrontation and rejection

You Feel:

- Guilt
- Pity
- Loss of respect
- Superiority

- Frustration
- Anger

Assertive Expression

Behavior:

- Stand up for their rights
- Won't violate others' rights
- Make demands using logic and control
- Take charge - insist they be heard
- All business, no play
- Negotiate honestly and openly

You Feel:

- Respected
- Valued
- Trusted

Defusing Anger 3-Step Process

1. **Recognize** the emotion – call it by name
2. **Apologize** - show you care – Actively listen and make a "no-fault apology."
3. **Solutionize** - Transition to Problem-Solving

The Active Listening Skills Review

- **Acceptance Responses** (*Okay, yes, I see*)
- **Clarifying Questions** (Move from generalizations to specifics)
- **Repeat** (Repeat verbatim a keyword or phrase)
- **Paraphrase** (Restate it in your own words)

- **Reflect** (emotion)
- **Summarize** (Paraphrasing in summary form, two or more topics or steps)

Problem-Solving Process Review

1. Separate the issues
2. Analyze the problem
3. Set Solution objectives
4. Set Criteria for success
5. Optional solutions
6. Select the best solution
7. Plan & Implement

8

Managing Customer Expectations

Create and Change Expectations Without Triggering Anger

Objectives

Managing expectations is usually a simple task of all parties agreeing on what is to be done and delivering on that agreement.

However, when unexpected complications occur, proactive communication, taking steps to prevent negative emotions, and engaging in previously agreed upon fallback plans, can all be used to impact the service recovery outcome.

The purpose of this chapter is to provide the following knowledge of how to:

- Set simple and complex expectations
- Ensure simple and complex expectations are met
- Manage project communications
- Use the steps to redefine expectations with "good" and "bad" news
- Prevent resetting unrealistic expectations from "good" news
- Minimize the potential for anger from "bad" news
- Debrief and evaluate the team's performance

Setting Expectations: Simple

Expectations are set in many ways, including:

- Directly stating an expectation.
- Through agreement.
- Inferring an expectation.
- Drawing a conclusion.
- Published literature.
- Track record.

The strength of the expectations can be influenced by:

- The prestige of the person stating, causing, or supporting the expectation.
- The length of time an expectation is allowed to stand – usually, the longer, the stronger.
- The number of times it is confirmed.

Setting expectations requires an understanding of:

- The customer's situation and requirements.
- Your capabilities and limitations.
- And your experiences with this customer.

Be clear about the expectations you set. **Often people hear what they want to hear!**

For example, if you were looking for "blue" items on a clothes rack, you could easily pick them out from those of a different color. Similarly, if you were looking for the good or the bad in someone, you could find it. Whatever you want or subconsciously need, you will set your filters to screen for it, and you will find it.

This means that people wanting and needing to hear a certain thing will listen for it. They will subconsciously set their filters to screen for it so that they can interpret it to mean what they want from what you say. Make sense? Be as clear as possible when setting even simple expectations.

Meeting Simple "Non-Standard" Expectations

Meeting expectations that vary from the "automatic routine standard" requires more attention. An informal project management process to define how these expectations will be met is necessary to prevent customer disappointment.

Basic project management steps that enable tracking and coordinating the necessary activities for any "non-standard" solution could include steps such as:

- Define the OUTCOME (solution, deliverable, result, etc.).
- List of WHAT needs to be done (action items) to achieve this solution outcome.
- Identify WHO will do each item
- Set start and end times/dates, identifying WHEN each item (or set of items) will be done.
- Define how you will MEASURE the extent to which a step or milestone has been achieved according to the specifications and expectations

A simple project management tracking form might include:

- Project Name:
- Team Leader:
- Deliverable/Outcomes:
- Action Items to achieve outcome:
- What to do:
- Who will do it:
- When will it be done:
- Measurement:
- Resources:

* A "deliverable" or "outcome is something the customer gets as part of the project.

If this is a routine project where you are responsible for most of the steps, simply list them in your calendar on the date they are to be done so that you have scheduled in time to get them completed by the due date.

Reference the project name in your calendar so you can always find the complete action planner in your files. For example, you might put "AB Co Radio Order Follow up" in your calendar for 10 AM on Tuesday. You could now look up the AB Co Radio Order checklist to see what that means, i.e., who will follow up, when, how you know it's being done, and how you will know when it's been done.

Setting Expectations: Complex

Anytime the item being ordered, or the service being requested, is not "off-the-shelf" or routine, expectations must be clarified. The more complex the project, the higher the need to manage it more formally and the expectations that go along with it.

Specifically, you would clarify and monitor:

- Customer's specifications, standards, and measures.
- Back-up plans.
- Who will do what, when, how with what resources, and in what time frame?
- The primary communications plan includes a distribution list, timing, and methods such as meetings, email, fax, etc.
- The process to follow should something need to change.

Understanding your customer's situation and requirements would include knowing:

- How will your performance be measured
- What aesthetic qualities (look, touch, and feel) does the customer expect

- Where you have leeway in such areas as delivery time or ability to substitute products
- Tolerance levels for uncertainties and other unknowns
- The types of pressures the customer is under and how that might influence their interpretation of what you said

Take the customer's point of view and ask, "What are the normal expectations of reasonable people in similar situations?" The "reasonable person test" would take into account such things as:

- How comparatively speaking, the competition could be expected to do in this situation. (Don't bring up or discuss this with the customer - this is an internal dialog.)
- What you (or your company's) reputation would lead a reasonable person to conclude.
- The person's previous experiences with others compared with you (and your company).
- Your experiences with this customer.

When setting expectations, recognize what you personally can do to fulfill the expectation and what is left for others to do. How you state what you can do and how you state what others will do can make a huge difference in the level of customer satisfaction that can result when an expectation is not met.

For example, even as simple as it sounds, just taking a phone call for someone and telling the caller that you will have the person return the call exceeds your capabilities. You cannot physically force another person to return a call. Instead, what you can do is pass the message on and "ask" the person to return the call.

Meeting Complex Expectations

Complex situations most likely will involve more comprehensive **project management strategies**, including such items as:

- Client:
- Project:
- Estimated project duration:
- Start date:
- Targeted end date:
- Project overview:
- The project team (with contact information):
- Comments:
- Assumptions upon which the work is undertaken
- Potential obstacles with "workaround" solutions:
- Project phases:
- Concept Phase
- Analysis Phase
- Design Phase
- Development Phase
- Delivery / Implementation Phase
- Evaluation Phase
- Significant milestones:
- Duration of steps and phases with start and end dates
- Action items identified and responsibilities assigned
- Resource requirements defined
- Deliverable defined
- Scheduled communications meetings
- Other items, as the project itself, dictate

To some extent, each situation will be different, and these factors would guide your choice of content and depth of the project management process.

Communication

Communicate proactively and consistently according to the expectations you have set. You do this by:

- Scheduling regular status reports
- Noting the routine content - what information will be included?
- Identifying the distribution list - who will get the information?
- Agreeing on the communications method(s) - e-mail, teleconference, etc.

Delivering "Good" News

Delivering "good news" ahead of routine status reports can easily set unrealistic expectations for the remaining action items. For example, suppose you received an earlier than expected shipment of products the customer has on back-order. While you may be tempted to call to tell them the good news, you might want first to check to see when they could be reasonably delivered. You don't want to get into a situation where the customer starts to pressure you for the products, potentially creating all sorts of bad feelings.

Include in these communications such information as:

- Content (what happened)
- Implications (meaning, impact on the rest of the project)
- Distribution list (who needs to know)
- Method(s) (how, i.e., email, teleconference)

Unless you know for sure, don't speculate on what this "good news" would mean for completing the rest of the project. You can imagine what it might be like to revisit the customer to take back your projections.

Delivering "Bad" News

A business reality is that unpredictable circumstances will throw a project or even an "off-the-shelf" solution "off course."

Deliver any news that will redefine expectations for the project at the earliest possible time. There are two sets of steps to take, the first set is done before you contact the customer, and the second set is done during the customer contact.

The steps to take before contacting the customer are:

1. Get the basic facts about what happened.
2. Identify the implications for both you and the customer to help you select the most workable solution.
3. Set a solution objective that meets or is as close to the original goal.
4. Explore optional solutions.
5. Select the most workable solution option.
6. Start the action plan for recovery.

And now, you are prepared to do the next step, which is contacting the customer.

When delivering news to customers that their expectations will not be met, they will naturally experience this as a loss. When a loss occurs, the grief process is triggered, and a natural part of that process is anger.

Therefore, when delivering news in which the customer might perceive a loss, the following method helps prevent triggering anger.

You can do this by quickly telling the customer the outline of what you want to talk about **before you actually discuss it.** This keeps the customer in suspense, so they don't know how to react until you get the complete information. When you end the discussion about what you want to talk about with a plan to minimize or negate the loss, the customer knows the end of the story (similar to someone telling the movie's outcome before you see it). The emotions are prevented from being experienced as intensely as they would have been, minimizing their expression as well.

The items to include in your outline when you contact the customer would be:

· That you encountered an unexpected challenge to the project in a specific area
· The implications of that challenge
· The solution objective
· The optional solutions you considered
· The solution you selected
· The plan you started to implement to correct the situation
· When you will follow up with them on the progress of the plan

Notice in the example below that no details about the problem or the implications are provided. If you initially provide details, you could get bogged down, allowing anger to surface. You want to get to the spoiler before that happens.

Let's look at an example acted out between Dave as the supplier, Nicky as Dave's supervisor, and Ray as the customer.

Ray answers the phone.

Ray: *"Box Car Company. This is Ray with the field engineering group. How can I help you?"*

Dave: *"Hi, Ray. This is Dave Smith."*

Ray: *"Hi, Dave. What's on your mind?"*

Dave: *"Ray, I wanted to get in touch with you to set a time to talk about the* **challenge we encountered** *with the programming part of the project.*

"Nicky and I want to review the **implications** *that will impact the timeline. I'd also like to brief you on the* **objective we've set**, *the* **options** *we discussed to* **narrow it down to the one** *we selected, and the* **plan of action we've implemented** *to correct and monitor the situation and get us back on track.*

"Do you have about 15 minutes to go over the high points, or do you want to set a phone appointment for later today?"

Ray: *"Dave, it sounds like you have it under control, so let's target 3 o'clock this afternoon to review the situation. And thank you for letting me know. Goodbye now.*"

In this example, Dave was able to provide Ray with an outline or agenda-style format of the information they would discuss at a later time. The outline brought a problem that could cause a potential loss and upset the customer. If the customer needed to be engaged in further problem-solving, that would also be part of the agenda-setting process.

The primary objective at this time is to minimize the impact of any loss. Dave did this by telling Ray they've figured out the problem, looked at the options, and decided to take action to get back on track, which can be interpreted as minimizing any potential loss.

That's why the conversation has to be in an outline or agenda style form with no specifics for the customer to get overly concerned about before you're ready for that discussion. Here, you just want to let them know that something came up, that you handled it, and potential loss will be minimal if any. They get to the end quickly, see that the outcome will be acceptable, and do so without having to grieve any real or imagined loss.

Debrief and Evaluate

For projects of any size, it is always a good learning strategy to engage the customer in a session to debrief the project.

This could be as simple as stating each expectation and asking the customer if those expectations were met to their satisfaction. Many companies now routinely conduct these types of brief surveys.

Debriefing more complex projects could involve an in-depth, step-by-step review of the project management system from an internal perspective to an in-depth "deliverable" versus "expectation" review with the client's project manager or the entire team.

Regardless of the project's complexity, you will always need to demonstrate and discuss how you met each customer's expectations. This can be done as a part of an internal team meeting or as a part of a professional development session.

Obviously, the better you understand what contributes to creating a satisfying experience for the customer, the more you will be able to strengthen customer loyalty.

Here's a simple survey to review to give you an idea about what one might look like.

"Mr., Mrs., _____ (customer name), I want to thank you for the opportunity to do business with you and your company. I have three quick questions about how you see our performance in fulfilling your order, is now a good time to do this, or should we set a phone appointment for later today?"

With approval,

"First, your order called for _____, to be delivered by _____ . Did your order arrive as expected in good condition?"

"Second, the item you ordered is designed to provide _____, _____, and _____. Are you finding that it does that to your satisfaction?"

"Is there anything else you can tell me about your order that you'd like us to know?

"Is there anything that you were especially pleased about?"

"Thank you very much, and we look forward to doing more business with you in the future."

The above question about what they liked about your product or service is critical in that it provides the customer the opportunity to rehearse and role-play what they might tell some other prospective customer. It helps them defend and talk positively about their purchase, reinforces their buying decision, creates a positive attitude, and builds loyalty. You get all this from a straightforward question.

Summary

As you can see, it's easy to set expectations. So easy that many are created just by who you are and what you do.

Setting complex expectations should be done with the process of managing them in mind. The project management process recommended in this chapter is straightforward and will handle most common projects. You'll most likely have someone trained in advanced project management methods to lead and monitor the project for larger projects.

Communications should be regularly scheduled with a preset standard agenda to guide the participant's expectations.

Good news, bad news: Without some forethought and care, delivering "good" news can inadvertently cause unrealistic expectations to be set.

Delivering "bad" news is an art form in and of itself. We discussed two sets of steps. The first set was to prepare you for the second set, which guides the actual customer content. The purpose of the second set is to prevent feelings of loss, which would trigger anger. The secret is to tell them what the movie's plot is, then tell them what happens in the end. When you tell them what happened, you've "spoiled" the film for them, and in so doing, they won't have the usual emotional ups and downs because they already know the end.

Ultimately, you'll want to debrief the project and evaluate how you met the customers' expectations. The outlined method will help ensure you learn from your experiences and that the next customer experience will be even better.

Job Aid - Managing Customer Expectations

Simple Expectations – Understand

- Customer's situation and requirements
- Your capabilities and limitations
- Your past experience with this customer

People hear what they want to hear!

Set Expectations By:

- Directly stating it
- Through agreement
- Inferring it

- Drawing conclusions
- Track record
- Published Information

Strength of Expectation based on:

- Prestige of person setting it
- Length of time it's been in place
- Number of times it's been confirmed

Set Complex Expectations –
Clarify and Monitor:

- Specifications, standards & measures
- Back up plans
- Action plan of who will do what, when, resources, time frame
- Primary Communications
- Distribution
- Timing
- Methods: meetings, email, fax,
- Change order process

Steps to Redefine Expectations

1. Get the basic facts
2. Identify the implications
3. Set the solution objective
4. Explore solution options
5. Select workable option
6. Start the plan for recovery
7. Contact the customer

Contact Customer Step

Prevent Loss & Anger

Quickly Lay out the following Agenda:

1. Encountered unexpected challenge
2. Implications
3. Solution objective
4. Optional solutions
5. Selected solution
6. Plan you initiated
7. Follow up plan
8. Questions?

Defusing Anger Review

1. Recognize
2. Apologize
3. Solutionize

9

Creating Customer Loyalty

Reduce costs and improve profits by creating long-term loyal customers

Objectives

Customer loyalty originates from your company's unique capabilities that help customers meet their needs better than your competitors can.

It is sustained by how well customers like interacting with those within your company.

Your professional interactions ultimately support high customer satisfaction ratings and high customer retention levels.

This chapter will provide you with basic and advanced knowledge, skills, and strategies to strengthen customer loyalty.

Learning and using these skills will reduce customer turnover and increase profitable long-term sales. Reduce costs of replacing customers, and improve profits from long-term customer retention.

After completing this chapter you will be able to:

- Define the key characteristics of a "loyal customer."
- Understand how doing the core customer engagement skills well forms the foundation for customer loyalty
- Know how to recover from a service misstep
- Know how to deliver bad news without upsetting the customer
- Create and strengthen customer loyalty attitudes

Overview

Creating and maintaining customer loyalty is a process in which you use basic and advanced skills.

The basic skills include professional methods to open and close conversations, ways to quickly establish trust and rapport, actively listen, solve problems, and defuse anger when called upon during service recovery situations.

You'll learn advanced skill sets to redefine a customer's expectations during a service failure and recovery, and you'll learn a powerful life skill of how to quickly create attitudes in your favor that are resistant to change.

Characteristics of Loyal Customers

Loyal customers are repeat buyers who consider us first as the source for meeting their needs. They are less price-sensitive, can defend you, and will enthusiastically recommend you to others with similar needs.

Repeat customers

- Consistently and competently apply unique capabilities to meet their fundamental human needs.
- Your unique capabilities are critical to the customers' success, resulting in customer loyalty.

Think of you first

- You are in an easily identifiable industry or have easy-to-identify capabilities.
- After the customer "defends" you, the emotional bond helps them remember us. You will learn how to do this in the section about creating attitudes.

Defend you

- Defending you (products, service, company) generates positive "attitudes" about us and supports repeat business.
- Defending your unique capabilities generates positive "attitudes" about how essential you are to them and locks in customer loyalty.
- Neutral to Positive to Champions.

Recommend you

- Demonstrate customer commitment and loyalty.
- Champion our cause.

Identifying customers who meet these characteristics will give you a better understanding of the result you will achieve by using the knowledge, skills, and strategies you will learn in this chapter.

Review these characteristics, and then identify three customers you know who have all of them.

Customer Engagement and Loyalty Building Skills

Creating customer loyalty is a skilled process in which you use your core and advanced skills.

The core or basic skills include professional methods to open and close a conversation, trust and rapport building, active listening, problem-solving, and defusing anger.

The advanced skill sets you'll learn to include how to redefine a customer's expectations during a service failure and recovery and the life skill of creating attitudes in your favor that are resistant to change.

Core Customer Interaction Skills

Let's start with business etiquette skills for opening and closing the conversation.

People who do exceptionally well in creating loyal customers establish their business relationships by using professional methods to open and close conversations.

Opening the Call or Contact Professionally

Your opening remarks should include:

1. Your company's name (or department if the call was transferred internally).
2. Your name, and
3. An offer to help.

For example, when making an offer to help, you might say, "How may I help you?"

Including these points in your greeting enables callers to know that they dialed the correct number and are talking with someone cheerfully prepared to be of assistance.

You can modify these remarks with comments such as:

"Thank you for calling." Or, if you're at reception or on the switchboard, you might ask, "How may I direct your call?"
   You could end with, "I'll transfer you now, and have a wonderful day."

If you're in the accounting department, you might answer, "Accounting department, this is Mary; how may I help you?"

Be sure to smile because this will communicate "welcome" in your voice.

Always, the FIRST and LAST thing a customer should hear or see from you is a smile that reassures the customer of the confidence you have about yourself and your company's ability to help.

Voice Tones

Opening and closing the conversation with the customer is always made with positive voice tones.

You create a positive professional impression when you:

Focus: Focus on the customer. Your sincere focused attention will be noticed. Put all other thoughts out of your mind except the customer's concerns.

Smile: Yes, a smile can be heard over the phone. Be enthusiastic about the mission you are carrying out.

Good posture: Good posture is comfortable and can produce alert, warm and friendly vocal overtones.

Articulate Clearly: Use a normal volume and speak clearly. Fewer misunderstandings will be your reward.

Positive Self-Talk: Tell yourself positive things about your ability to understand your customer's point of view, stresses, and concerns, and this will come across to the person on the other end of the phone.

You Create NEGATIVE TONES and severely damage your professionalism and customer relationships when you:

Distracted: When you seem distracted. People can tell when your full attention is not focused on them. Hold a side conversation, and you will evoke a negative emotional response and trigger a loss of trust.

Don't Smile: When you don't smile. Your tone often sounds flat or disinterested.

Slouch: Breathing can be affected to the extent that the power goes out of your voice.

Mumble Words: It's difficult enough to hear anything at a busy and noisy facility. With lazy speech habits, you add to anxiety, building miscommunications.

Negative Self-Talk: What you tell yourself about yourself and the customer will most definitely come across in your tone of voice and will be reflected in your effectiveness in being of assistance.

Reflect on how you opened a call in the past with the customer you selected above that met the characteristics of a loyal customer.

- Did you Smile and use positive voice tones?
- Did you state your company name or department?
- Did you introduce yourself?
- Did you make an offer to help?

End the Call or Contact Professionally

To end the call or contact professionally and efficiently:

- Use the caller's name. People stop and pay attention when they hear their name.
- Review what you've accomplished on this call in a positive way using the past tense. Talking in the past tense starts them thinking about the call being over.
- State the next steps to confirm that you and the customer understand what will happen next.
- Verify that all concerns have been addressed. This signals that this part of the call is at an end and brings them back on track if other issues need to be addressed.

Reflect on how you ended a call with the customer you selected.

- Did you use the customer's name?
- Did you review what you accomplished using the past tense?
- Did you state the next steps?
- Did you verify that all concerns were addressed?

Even if you checked yes to each of these, were there any you want to do better? If so, how?

Establishing Trust and Rapport – Quick Review

There are specific methods that you can use to establish trust and rapport.

These methods include:

- Finding Common Ground
- Pacing and Leading

- Establishing Credentials
- Creating a Psychological Truth.

Common Ground: Find what you have in common with them, such as weather, traffic, business goals, etc. Stay away from politics, religion, sex, and sometimes sports.

Pacing and Leading: Mirror and match what you observe them doing, including dress, posture, speech (rate, tone, cadence), breathing, etc. Then lead by changing any of these.

Credentials: Your position, background experience, knowledge and skills, special certifications, and so on.

Psychological Truth: Understand them first. If you sincerely try to understand another person's point of view first, they become psychologically obligated to try to understand yours. How? Use active listening skills.

Which of these methods do you use most often?

Active Listening Skills – Quick Review

Your Active Listening skills are some of the most critical communications skills you can possess. Your effectiveness goes up dramatically as you become more skilled in using them.

Most people already know these listening skills. But what we don't do as well as we could, is to use them when we need to ensure the right work gets done right and use them to prevent misunderstandings. Except for asking clarifying questions, you're not adding new content to the interaction; you are providing feedback to the speakers as though you are a mirror.

The more comfortable you become using them, the more likely you will use them when they are needed.

Practice with family and friends, as well as with co-workers and customers. You'll have fun with this and learn a lot about how to use them most effectively.

Remember that not all six skills are used in all situations. Just be sure to use the appropriate ones when that is what you should do.

Active Listening Skills

- Acceptance Responses
- Asking Clarifying Questions
- Repeating keywords/phrases
- Paraphrasing content
- Reflecting emotion
- Summarizing

Acceptance Responses: Acceptance responses are simple and brief words such as "Yes," "I see," "Uh-huh," "Okay," "Go on," "Tell me more," and so on. Use acceptance responses to let the speaker know you're listening without interrupting their flow of thought.

Asking Clarifying Questions: Ask clarifying questions to clear up any points that might be misinterpreted. When unsure you understood correctly, ask questions to clarify that you heard it right.

Asking these questions is not only in the asking, but also in knowing what to ask. This speaks to your credentials.

Repeating keywords/phrases: Highlight keywords or phrases that indicate you have identified the most critical components of the message.

Frequent misunderstandings occur with number sequences (phone, credit card, PO), addresses, words with double meanings ("here" and "hear"), and specific step-by-step instructions. These all bear repeating.

Paraphrasing content: Paraphrasing is saying what you thought you heard in your own words.

Often, people begin the paraphrase with statements such as:

- *Let me make sure I understood what you said.*
- *So, as I understand it,*

Reflecting emotion: To let the speaker know that you are aware of the feelings they are experiencing, you need to mention them in your feedback. You do this by naming the emotion or expressing the same sentiment in your voice and mannerisms. Your ability to recognize and reflect emotion is one of the most critical skills when working with stressful situations.

For example, for negative emotions, you might reflect, "That's got to be frustrating." "I'm sorry that happened to you." "I can see why you're upset." Or "Argh." On the positive side, "How exciting for you." "You're going to love this." "I'm glad that worked out for you."

Summarizing: Summarizing the conversation assures both the listener and speaker that a complex message was received and understood. Summarizing uses all the other active listening skills. The difference between paraphrasing and summarizing is that you paraphrase one topic and summarize multiple topics.

When was the last time you paraphrased content or reflected emotion?

Problem-Solving – Quick Review

Using a systematic problem-solving model that consistently gets positive results is an invaluable tool.

Problem-solving is what you do automatically many times every day. There is no question about your problem-solving abilities. Can you define your process so others can learn and your team can have a consistent, reliable, and analyzable series of steps?

Excelling with this skill set helps you excel with your customers.

We've selected a standard customer service problem-solving model that can handle the most straightforward or the most complex problems you might face.

The steps are:

1. Separate the issues.
2. Analyze the "presenting problem."
3. Determine the solution objective.
4. Define the criteria for success.
5. Develop optional solutions.
6. Select the optimal solution.
7. Plan, implement, and evaluate.

Step 1. Separate the Issues: It's not uncommon for customers to have multiple issues. Separate them so you can work on the one that will solve the most number at once. Separate the emotions and defuse them as appropriate.

Step 2. Presenting Problem: Customers present problems as they see them interfering with their goals, not as root causes of the problems (or the real problem). You may not be able to solve the root cause of the problem. Work on the problems at the level you can solve that will resolve the greatest number of issues.

For example, late shipping may be due to a shortage of workers or the wrong address. Which can you solve?

Step 3. Solution Objective: What outcome will solve the problem and satisfy the customer?

What can we do to meet the customer's objectives within company guidelines?

Consider both the customer's expectations and requirements within the confines of your capabilities and constraints.

These considerations can influence how the solution objective is stated and agreed upon.

Step 4. Success Criteria: How does the customer define a successful resolution of the presenting problem? How do you define success?

Achieving a clearly written "solution objective" is a clear indication of success.

Include defusing negative emotions as part of the criteria, or you might get a satisfied angry customer rather than a loyal one.

Step 5. Optional Solutions: There are usually multiple solutions to most problems.

If this is a recurring problem that cannot be prevented, then you will have a standard solution with some variables to suggest as options. Brainstorm with the customer to come up with acceptable optional solutions.

Step 6. Optimal Solution: Summarize the top solutions, and if all things are equal, let the customer choose the solution to implement.

Step 7. Plan – Implement – Evaluate: Who will do what, when, and with what resources? How will we know it's been done and is successful? If not, revisit the problem definition, solution objective, criteria, and selection.

How will follow-up be done with the customer so we can continue to develop a loyal customer?

Defusing Anger – Quick Review

Anger provides the energy to overcome obstacles that block a person's ability to meet their needs.

Loss of not getting these needs met means there will be anger to provide the energy to stop or reverse the loss. When a loss is perceived, real or imagined; past, present, or future, anger will be evoked to provide the energy to stop and reverse the loss.

Intensity can range from annoyance to rage.

In many customer service situations, the problem the customer is contacting you about is already causing a loss or threatening to cause a loss if it's not solved.

Angry people want three things:

1. They want you to recognize their anger.
2. They want to know that you care that they're upset.
3. They want you to help them stop the loss, reverse it, and prevent it from happening again.

Let's look at these steps in greater detail so you'll know how to use them.

First, the person wants you to recognize that they are upset. Ignoring it will only serve to cause it to become more intense.

Use your Active Listing Skill of Reflecting Emotion.

As soon as **you name it, you defuse it**. However, it won't stay gone unless you continue with the following two steps.

Second, the person **wants someone to care** about what's happening to them. We all would. They automatically go into sadness when the anger is released.

One effective way is to apologize for what they're going through. A no-fault apology is one in which you are not taking responsibility; you're simply sorry this is happening to them or to anyone.

For example, you might say, "I'm very sorry this happened . . ."

You must be sincere and authentic for this to be effective. Phony won't work. You simply must care about the person as a human being in need of your help.

However, do not sympathize. Your feelings of pity will come out.

Do not feel their pain as an Empath would. It will wear you out.

Instead, they want you to understand their feelings and their right to them. Do that, and you'll be most effective.

Third, the person wants someone to **help them stop the loss**. Even reverse it, and hopefully, prevent it from happening again. Again, this step happens automatically.

You do this by problem-solving. For example, you could introduce the first step in the process by saying, "Let's separate these two issues and tackle them one at a time."

This process works well because it fits within other methods and skill sets you've learned in this book.

1. You established a business relationship through your professional opening remarks, and your offer to help invites the customer to begin the conversation.
2. Your ability to rapidly establish trust and rapport by first pacing their intensity and then leading them to a calmer sense of being.
3. Using Active Listening skills will help establish a Psychological Truth that will position you to handle the rest of the conversation.
4. Your use of the Defusing Anger process, which starts with the Active Listening Skill of Reflecting Emotion, further demonstrates your insight.
5. You are now positioned to show you care using your no-fault apology and moving into professional-level problem-solving.

Points to keep in mind

- You may have to go through the defusing anger process more than once. As the person relives the triggering event, negative emotions may reignite. That's okay. Just repeat the three steps.
- Err on the side of being more upset than less. You would not want to say, Oh, it's not that bad.
- Making it seem less than it is will intensify the emotion and block further communication.
- If you are uncertain about the intensity of the emotion, then err on the side of greater intensity. For example, "from what you've said, if that happened to me, I'd really be upset."
- Now let the customer confirm or tell you it's not that bad. This will further defuse the emotion.

- During customer interaction, focus on what you and the customer CAN DO rather than can't do. If you catch yourself saying, "CAN'T...," **follow it immediately** by saying what you CAN DO to avoid creating loss and triggering anger.

To help remember the steps use the rhyming words:

- Recognize, Apologize, Solutionize.
- Recognize, Apologize, Solutionize.
- Recognize, Apologize, Solutionize.

Advanced Loyalty Building Skills

The following two segments will provide you with advanced skills to support your role in creating and keeping loyal customers.

The first is part of a service recovery system. When service failure occurs, and the customer must be made aware of the situation, this segment will teach you how to deliver the bad news in such a way as to minimize any negative impact on your relationship.

The second is a life skill that will teach you how to create attitudes that are resistant to change. You'll be surprised how easy it is and how often both good and bad attitudes are unintentionally created in different areas of your life.

Service Recovery - Delivering Bad News – Quick Review

You know from the Defusing Anger segment that when a person experiences loss, real or imagined, past, present, or future, anger will emerge to provide the added energy needed to stop the loss.

During a service failure, no matter how small, if the customer is not getting what they expected, then the customer will experience loss.

That means you will want to do everything possible to minimize the perception and feeling of loss.

The procedure to deliver bad news and reset the customer's expectations follows a strategy to prevent feelings of loss and anger.

There are two phases to this process. Phase one is internal problem-solving, and Phase two is contacting the customer.

Phase One: The first thing you want to do when you become aware of a service failure with one of your customers is to:

1. Get the facts. You need to know with some degree of certainty what you're talking about. No miscommunication.
2. Identify the implications. How will this impact the customer? The more serious and negative the impact, the more you need to involve others on your team.

The next steps you recognize are from the problem-solving model you reviewed earlier in this book.

1. Set the solution objective. What needs to happen?
2. Explore solution options. How can you make it happen?
3. Select the most workable solution. If you need the customer involved with this step, start what you can for the next step. You want a flow of action started when you talk with the customer.
4. Start the action plan for recovery. The customer will feel more confident in your abilities to make things right.
5. Contact the customer – this begins Phase Two of the process.

Phase Two: Contact the Customer. When delivering bad news, you'll want to do so in such a way that helps minimize the feeling of loss.

You do this by providing the customer with the plan or outline of what you want to discuss before discussing the details.

This keeps the customer in suspense so that they don't react until you get the full information.

Tell them:

1. That you have encountered an unexpected challenge to the project in a specific area.
2. The implications of that challenge. For example, what that means to the service delivery
3. Set solution objective. For example, you still want to meet the timeline.
4. You explored all the reasonable options. Here you want to convey that you've covered them all so the customer doesn't start second-guessing by asking have you tried this? Have you tried that?
5. Select the solution option that keeps you on track and that the plan is being implemented to correct the situation. If you need customer input, now is the time to include that in your agenda.
6. Let them know you have a follow-up plan to keep them aware of the progress made on the plan. This step can be included in your action plan and not as a separate agenda item.
7. Ask for an appointment or if they have time now to review this informa-tion.

For Example, John is the customer and answers the call.

"Hello John, this is Bob DeGroot. I'm the service representative for XYZ Company."

John might respond with, *"Yes, Bob, what can I do for you?"*

Now you would set the agenda and then ask for time to discuss the items. For example, this service rep might say,

"I wanted to get in touch with you as soon as possible to let you know that we've encountered an unexpected challenge with the programming part of the project. I also want to talk about the implications of that challenge, the options we've discussed internally, the direction we're going, and the plan of action we've implemented to correct the situation. Do you have about 15 minutes to go over the high points now, or do you want to set a phone appointment for later today?"

As you can see, by setting the agenda first, you can prevent or minimize as much customer perceived loss as possible to prevent strong negative emotions from erupting.

If they do get upset, you also now know how to defuse the emotion.

Creating Loyalty Attitudes – Quick Review

The customer becomes loyal when they believe your unique capabilities add significant value to their ability to meet their needs and that you can do so better than the competitors can.

That uniqueness could include characteristics of your company's products and services, how your company does business, and the unique or distinctive capabilities of the leadership and staff.

Beliefs can change with new credible information. Attitudes, however, are resistant to change even in the face of significant credible contradictory information.

Therefore, our objective is to convert changeable beliefs about our unique capabilities into change-resistant attitudes.

You create an attitude by connecting the targeted BELIEF with an EMOTION!

Creating attitudes follows the simple formula:

$$\textbf{B}\text{elief} + \textbf{E}\text{motion} = \textbf{A}\text{ttitude}$$
$$\textbf{B} + \textbf{E} = \textbf{A}$$

You create emotions by challenging the desired belief or behavior with some form of the question, "Why!?"

The "exclamation point" makes the why question a challenge rather than just a question of curiosity.

The challenge "Why" evokes the DEFENSE emotions. It causes the person to defend the belief or behavior. This combines the belief about your unique capabilities with the defense emotion, thereby creating an attitude.

Therefore, it stands to reason that the more frequently they are challenged, the stronger the challenges become and the stronger their attitude will be.

Take care not to overdo it. They must win. Make the initial challenges gentle, full of curiosity, and even indirect.

For example, for our purposes, you can use different ways to ask "why," such as "how did you come to that conclusion," "what made you decide to do it that way," and "when did that first become important," and so on.

Process & Examples

To make the process of creating attitudes even more manageable, there is a simple procedure where you first orient the customer to the targeted belief or behavior, support it, gently challenge it, and then support it again.

Look at these examples to illustrate the pattern used to establish attitudes. Recognize that these are oversimplified and that the steps are often integrated into a more extensive dialog.

Orient & Support the Targeted Belief or Behavior: "That's great that you're using the _____ (unique capability)."
   Challenge gently: "What made you choose that option?"
   Support again: "I like how you decided that. It makes sense."

Orient & Support: "I really like to use _____ (unique capability)."
   Challenge gently: "Why was that important to you?"
   Support again: "That's really important. I hadn't thought about it that way. Thank you."

Orient & Support: "Thank you for choosing us as your supplier."
   Challenge gently: "What were your top reasons for choosing us?"
   Support again: "I'm very pleased to hear that. Thank you. We look forward to working with you to meet those needs."

Why did you do that? Oops!

When do people usually challenge beliefs or behaviors with the common question, *"Why did you do that?"*

Do they ask that question when the person did something good or bad?

What does the person have to defend, good behavior or bad behavior?

What's being created, good attitudes or bad attitudes?

Easy to do, isn't it? You're doing it already and have most of your life. So be careful about what you challenge, or you might get the opposite of what you want.

- Challenge only the beliefs or behaviors you want, and never challenge those you don't want.
- Challenge only what you can provide as unique capabilities, and never challenge what you cannot provide.
- Challenge only what you want to happen with increased intensity and frequency

This is the primary process of creating and embedding corporate, family, and personal values.

You are given the value and then put it to the test, where you are challenged by someone else or even by yourself to defend it. Often, this is the defining moment for accepting or rejecting a belief or value.

The process then is to catch the person doing something right or bring the desired belief or behavior up in a discussion so that when you orient the person to the targeted belief or behavior, it makes clear what you are challenging.

The formula is simply to Orient & Support, Challenge gently, and then Support again.

Countering Bad Attitudes – Quick Review

You can counter, cover, isolate, or change "bad" attitudes in several ways. Think each of them through. You might rehearse and combine a couple of ways that work better for your interaction style. With any method you select, **always start by establishing strong rapport.**

Create Stronger Opposing Attitudes

One way to create counterbalancing attitudes is to wait until they exhibit the correct behavior, orient supportively, gently challenge, and help them win. Close the process by supporting them again. Rinse and repeat several times, coming from different directions.

Remember, you're taking their current attitude, no matter how strong, and deeming it the weaker one, so you can help them build a stronger one to counterbalance it.

Role Reversal

Another way to weaken a strong attitude toward doing bad behavior is to conduct a role reversal session. The point, counter-point debate style works well – especially with group behavior you'd like to see change. In this procedure, the person (or team) is assigned to research and develop the best arguments they can that are counter to their current attitude. At the same time, you (team B or someone you assign) should prepare to argue the person's (with a bad attitude) views, opinions, and arguments.

Surround the Target Attitude with Conflicting Attitudes

Following the "Cognitive Dissonance" idea, identify two or three beliefs or behaviors that express the same core value that counters the attitude you want to change. For example, your attitude countering strategy for coming late to work might be saying, "I know this isn't who you are. These could just be isolated times for you. But, clear something up for me. Why do you see yourself as someone on which I can rely? Why do you think I can depend on you to do what you say you will do?"

Parallel Beliefs or Behaviors

You can also surround the target attitude with more superficial and concrete beliefs or behaviors than dealing at the core values level.

For example, *"If it's okay for you to be late for work, then why is it not okay for you to be late for a movie, your date, doctor, dentist, or _____?"*

"If it's okay for you to embarrass others (me) when you _____, why is it not okay for them (me) to embarrass you in front of your friends by doing the same thing to you? Why is it not a good thing to intentionally embarrass _____?"

Using this reversal is a little tricky. You know the person you'll be challenging. Think about the types of answers they could throw back. If they don't defend doing the right thing, rework the question until it gets what you want.

Summary

Customer loyalty originates from your company's unique capabilities that help customers meet their needs better than your competitors can.

It is sustained by how well customers like interacting with those within your company.

Your professional interactions ultimately support high customer satisfaction ratings and high customer retention levels.

Job Aid – Creating Customer Loyalty

KEY CHARACTERISTICS

- Repeat customers
- Think of you first
- Less price sensitive
- Defend you
- Recommend you

BASIC SKILLS

- Open & Close Conversation

- Trust $ Rapport Building
- Active Listening Skills
- Defusing Customer Anger
- Problem-Solving Model

ADVANCED SKILLS

- Service Recovery
- Internal Problem-Solving
- Wins – 30 seconds each
- Creating Attitudes
- Belief + Emotion = Attitude (B=E=A)
- Orient and Support – Challenge – Support

10

Stress Control

A Life Skill to Keep You Healthy

Objectives

Stress control is a life skill that will help keep medical costs down, reduce turnover, improve relationships, reduce errors, reduce accidents, and dramatically improve customer perceptions of service competency. Show a customer how stressed you are, and you'll raise their anxieties about your competency to do the job.

Numerous research studies show that 75% to 90% of all visits to primary care physicians are for stress-related issues. Stress also intensifies symptoms and slows recovery.

In this chapter, you'll learn the mental, emotional, and physical signs of stress. You'll also learn the five phases of the stress response process and several effective coping methods in each phase. And, you'll develop a personal "stress control plan" to fit your exact needs.

The purpose of this chapter is to provide the knowledge to:

- Identify sources of work-related stress
- Recognize the signs and symptoms of stress
- Understand the stress response process
- Learn effective coping strategies for each stage in this process
- Use this process to guide you when you develop a stress control plan of action for the stress in your life

Overview

Stress is the result of external and internal events called stressors. These stressors cause you to adapt in some way or experience consequences that may not suit you. Finding a healthy and effective way to adapt is called coping.

For example, trees cope with the high wind by bending and swaying to relieve the pressure.

Not everyone experiences the same events in the same way. Something that causes you stress may have a calming or no effect on another.

While you may be unable to change the stressors, you can change how you respond to it.

Stress is cumulative, and adding one stressor on top of another can get weighted down until your coping skills are no longer effective.

When coping skills break down, people often revert to some earlier method of successful coping such as getting angry or throwing a tantrum. That's why it is essential to identify the causes of your stress, understand how they affect you, and then develop plans to deal with each one effectively.

Finally, short-term stress is easier to handle than long-term stress. Intense, long-term stress can lead to fatigue, difficulty sleeping, and other potentially harmful symptoms. That's why taking time away from stressful situations is so important. That means you should take breaks, have lunch outdoors, and take vacations without work. You must periodically and routinely let your body and mind recover.

Workplace Stressors

While this chapter focuses on the stressors and coping strategies used in the work setting, be assured that the principles apply to all areas of life.

Stressors in the work setting can be organized into four primary categories.

- Environmental
- Job/Task Demands
- Organizational Factors
- Career Issues

The intensity of the effects will vary from none to significant. Some stressors may be constant, some may be infrequent, and some will be non-existent. The list is comprehensive but not exhaustive – meaning others may not be on the list. Identify those areas that cause you stress. You might make a mental note about the extent to which each is present in your job and how you cope with it.

Environmental Stressors

- Noise pollution
- Ergonomic design deficiencies (office layout, furniture, etc.)
- Temperatures (too hot, too cold)
- Air - ventilation (stuffy)
- Pollutants (smoke, chemicals)
- Lighting (too high, too low)
- Isolation or crowding

Job/Task Demands

- Excessive or inadequate workload
- Excessive hours
- Shift work

- Low control over workload
- Pace (too fast, too slow)
- High responsibility/low authority
- Holding down more than one job
- Insufficient resources to do the job
- Problems are beyond your control

Organizational Factors

- The ambiguity of role functions, scope, and purpose
- Unclear job objectives
- Unclear job expectations
- Low participation in decisions affecting job
- Interpersonal relationships with supervisors
- Inadequate support from supervisors
- Ineffective performance by supervisors
- Conflict and ambiguity about what's expected.
- Poor relationships with coworkers
- Politics overrides performance

Career Issues

- The ambiguity of job future
- Over/under promotion
- Status confusion
- Job obsolescence
- Early retirement
- Low job security

Keep a running list of things that cause you to experience stress. Developing effective coping strategies will involve the cause of the stress if it's known. Recognize that the cause may not be work-related but comes from other areas of your life.

Life Stressors

While our focus thus far has been on work-related stress, it's important to look at other areas of your life where stress could be present. These areas could include:

- Personal (mental, physical, spiritual)
- Family (immediate, relatives)
- Social (friendships, networks, events)
- Professional (education, career path)
- Financial (income, debt, wealth management, retirement)
- Possessions (car, house, boat, computer, bicycle, clothes)
- Lifestyle (modern, conservative, country, urban, suburban, sophisticated, stylish)
- Activities (commute, events, commitments)

Again, the stress could be intermittent, constant, non-existent, or intense.

Signs and Symptoms of Stress

Every person will experience stress during their lifetime. Not all stress is bad. Some stress is helpful to motivate us, and some people with good coping skills seem to thrive on certain stress levels.

However, signs and symptoms of stress will begin to show without applying effective coping skills. Often, they are gradual and hard to notice, while at other times, they are "in your face" obvious.

Symptom Categories

- Emotional

- Cognitive
- Physical
- Interpersonal Relations
- Behavioral

Just as people experience stressors in different ways, they also show different signs and symptoms, from mild to severe. Keep track of the types of stressors and intensity of the signs and symptoms you experience. Let's take a closer look at each of these categories.

Emotional

- Increased anxiety
- Depression or sadness are frequent experiences
- Feelings of helplessness and hopelessness
- Efforts seem futile, leading to a negative outlook
- Irritability
- Anger or fear emerge ("fight" or "flight")
- Low self-esteem damages self-perception
- Impulsive actions, impatient and unstable behavior are common
- Frustration increases
- Sense of humor decreases
- Little things interpreted as bothersome
- The feeling of control over things is less frequent

Cognitive

- Distractibility increases
- Concentration ability decreases
- Remembering is difficult; forgetfulness common
- Errors increase
- Reasoning abilities decrease
- Disorganization increases

- Negative thoughts increase
- Irresponsible behavior and poor decisions increase
- A paycheck is the only reward for working

Physical

- Tensing of muscles (neck and shoulders)
- Increased heart rate
- Increased blood pressure
- Headaches
- Increased perspiration
- Dilation of pupils and widening of eyes
- Indigestion
- Increased energy and alertness
- Increased use of the restroom
- Lowered immune system, more susceptible to colds and flu
- Allergies increase
- Lethargy, depletion, exhaustion

Interpersonal Relationships

- Becoming irritable, quick-tempered, quarrelsome
- Insensitivity toward the needs of others
- Self-sacrifice (working longer hours)
- Sex life suffers
- Communications seem strained
- No time for friends, relationships suffer
- Dependencies increase

Behavioral

- Sleeping habits change
- Errors at work increase
- Drinking or smoking increase
- Appearance suffers
- Eating habits change (overeating or under eating)
- Accidents or anxiety about accidents increase
- Absence from work increases
- Sabotage or counterproductive activities occur at work
- Fatigue leads to depletion of energy, commitment, dedication, etc.
- Creativity and productivity decrease

From time to time, most of us will experience some of these symptoms at varying intensity levels in response to stressful events. That's a normal part of life. However, when the stressor remains constant, your reaction (symptoms) is continuous, then damage can occur. This is what you want to minimize.

Stress Response Process

The stress response you experience will also become the outline you will use to build effective coping mechanisms.

So, let's first get familiar with what you go through when you experience stress.

There are five stages in the Stress Response Process.

1. Triggering Event
2. Cognitive Appraisal
3. Emotional Response
4. Physical Response
5. Behavioral Response

Let's review each stage and examine some successful coping strategies others have used.

1. **Triggering Event:** This is the event that demands adaptation. The event can be real or imagined and located in the past, present, or future.

2. **Cognitive Appraisal:** This is the often-instantaneous Appraisal of the event's impact on you. You then label it as "good" or "bad." This step in the process is related to your value system. If the event is highly emotional, and you have a previous negative experience with this or even a vaguely similar event, then the cognitive Appraisal can be automatically bypassed. This would then result in an immediate emotional response.

3. **Emotional Response:** This stage can be strong or weak, positive or negative. "Strong" positive or negative emotions often override the cognitive reasoning process. If this happens, we can become irrational or do things we wouldn't consider doing. Changing how we think about the event (cognitive Appraisal), and finding the silver lining, will change how we feel about the event. Change your thinking to change your emotion.

4. **Physical Response:** This stage can be responsible for many changes in the body. The circulatory and muscular systems are most likely to be affected. The large muscles are tensed and made ready, and the blood flow is restricted to surface areas in the case of injury. Further, our bodies respond by providing energy sources and chemicals to meet the challenge of change. With long-term stress, some chemicals produced from the adrenal gland, such as cortisol, can cause belly fat to accumulate.

5. **Behavioral Response:** This stage occurs when a verbal or non-verbal action occurs, such as meeting with a person in authority or going for a walk. It may have adverse effects on you, like overeating, or positive effects, like beginning an exercise program.

Coping Strategies

Stress is inevitable, and we must all prepare to cope. Coping strategies help get control of the stress response process. ***The earlier the coping method is used, the more effective it is.***

Sometimes you can develop a single coping strategy in one area to deal with several stressors at once, and sometimes, you will need to develop a specific coping mechanism with a single stressor. Select something that is causing you stress right now, and then select the coping strategies in the Stress Response Process for each stage that would be right for you. Use these strategies to build your own *Plan of Action to Control Stress*

Triggering Events – real or imagined; past, present, future

Find those things that irritate you that you can control and deal with them now. Set up some way to prevent them from happening in the future.

- Stop the event before it happens.
- Avoid the event.
- Fix, replace, or get rid of things (events) that stress you.
- Get help (counseling) with upsetting relationships.
- Change how you perceive, think, and talk about an event.
- Learn and practice a different response to the event.
- Use the stressor as "exercise" to strengthen your ability to handle stress.
- Take periodic breaks from stressors (build stamina).

Cognitive Appraisal - instantaneous evaluation of the event as good or bad

If you can't stop the event from triggering your stress response process, the next stage will be to decide how it agrees or conflicts with your belief and value systems. It can be harmful or good, depending upon your Appraisal.

Your Appraisal is influenced by your past experiences, values, choices, and priorities in life. Know what's important to you and what's not.

- Good thing or bad thing decision usually happens automatically, so practice responding to similar stressors in a more desired way.
- Develop and fully explore viable options. Find a way to make an option better than the current situation.
- Ask, "What's the worst thing that could happen?" Prepare options.
- Now, what's the good that can come from this experience? Find the good and focus on it.
- Stop the negative thoughts. Change how you perceive, think, and talk about the event. Change your thinking to change your emotions in Step 3. Start looking forward to the event. Look for the fun, the good, the positive, and live that experience.

CAUTION: Do not continue to rethink the situation in negative terms. This will only serve to re-excite your stress response and cause more and more Adrenalin to be pumped into your system.

Emotional Response – strong emotions interfere with rational thought

At this stage, you are starting to feel the emotions related to your cognitive Appraisal of "good" or "bad."

However, you might note that if the event is one or similar to one that has been experienced before, you may automatically bypass the cognitive appraisal stage.

- Be aware of your feelings. To change what you're feeling, change what you're thinking.
- Laugh; be around happy things, people, or situations. If you want to be happy, sometimes you must act happy until you feel happy.
- Call on your support network.
- Talk it out and allow yourself to view different perspectives.
- Release emotions in a safe place.

CAUTION: In many companies, unleashing strong emotions around co-workers, supervisors, and others can be career-limiting.

Physical Response – move your body

Emotions cause the release of chemicals throughout the body. These chemicals cause physiological changes such as breathing rate, muscle tension, heart rate, and many other physiological responses. The goal of your coping strategies at this stage is to reverse these effects.

- Take six deep breaths. Breathe in through your nose and out through pursed lips. Relax and tell yourself you are feeling calm.
- Get up and move! Take a quick two or three-minute walk.
- Tense and release (gently tense and release major muscles in your body, including the neck, shoulders, arms, hands, legs, and feet.
- Stretch and move stiff muscles.

- Use mental Imagery to get completely relaxed. Just imagine yourself in a safe place. Breathe in deeply and slowly, and as you exhale, imagine each of your muscle groups beginning to relax. Start with your facial muscles and work down to your feet.

Behavioral Response – take decisive action

At this stage in the stress response process, you are now about to take some action to help reduce the stressor's effects.

You may also choose to adapt and accept the change while making plans to prevent this stressor from happening again.

- The action we take is most effective when directly related to the stressor.
- Make a list of actions — set priorities.
- Manage tasks. Once your list is complete, stop adding. If time and resources are available, you can replace a current completed item with a new item.
- Be assertive (not aggressive) with the offending party.
- Talk with an authority that can influence the stressor (event, condition, etc.).
- Hold a meeting with those involved to problem solve and plan action.
- Take steps to prevent a recurrence.
- Implement one of your viable options.
- Adapt and accept the change.

This step concludes your plan. You may want to make sure you have it recorded so you can review it as you implement your selected strategies.

Plan of Action to Control Stress

Identify the signs and symptoms each time you find something causing you stress. Reducing the prevalence and intensity can be used to measure your coping success. For example, you could give each symptom a low, medium, or high rating. Then after you've implemented your plan, measure them again. This is a great way to build confidence in your growing collection of effective coping strategies.

- Identify the stressor and the signs and symptoms
- Review each stage of the Stress Response Process and select appropriate coping strategies.

1. Triggering Event: something happens – prevent, avoid, fix, replace
2. Cognitive Appraisal: you decide good or bad – change how you perceive it, develop viable options
3. Emotional Response: negative or positive – change your emotion by changing your thinking
4. Physical Response: fight or flight chemicals released in the body – deep breathing, getting up and move
5. Behavioral Response: take action – list actions, set priorities, implement
6. Implement and measure results.

Summary

Workplace Stressors

- Environmental (noise, air quality, lighting, crowding, etc.)
- Job / Task Demands (workload, pace, control, resources, etc.)
- Organizational Factors (ambiguity in role, objectives, expectations, etc.)
- Career Issues (ambiguity of job future, worth, security, etc.)

Life Stressors

- Personal (mental, physical, spiritual)
- Family (immediate, relatives)
- Social (friendships, networks, events)
- Professional (education, career path)

- Financial (income, debt, wealth management, retirement)
- Possessions (car, house, boat, computer, bicycle, clothes)
- Lifestyle (modern, conservative, country, urban, suburban, sophisticated, stylish)
- Activities (commute, events, commitments)

Symptoms

- Behavioral (sleep, errors, appearance, fatigue, etc.)
- Interpersonal (insensitive, no time for friends, etc.)
- Physical (increased heart rate, blood pressure, and respiration)
- Cognitive (increased distractibility, decreased concentration, etc.)
- Emotional (increased anxiety, sadness, irritability, frustration, etc.)

Stress Response Process

1. Triggering Events – something happens
2. Cognitive Appraisal – you decide whether it is good or bad
3. Emotional Response – negative or positive
4. Physical Response – fight or flight chemicals released in the body
5. Behavioral Response – talk and take action

Coping Strategies

1. Triggering Event – prevent, avoid, fix, replace
2. Cognitive Appraisal – change how you perceive it, develop viable options
3. Emotional Response – change the emotion by changing the thinking
4. Physical Response – deep breathing, get up and move
5. Behavioral Response – list actions, set priorities, implement

You now have the knowledge and strategies to identify and cope with most of the stress you'll experience in your life. You know you must consciously practice them if you want them to be available to you during intense stress. Select and write down three to five stressors each month and put them through this process. Measure your results.

I felt unusual business-related stress not long ago and immediately engaged in this process. By the time I finished writing down and trying the coping strategies I selected, the stress had diminished from a medium level of intensity to almost non-existent. Going into a problem-solving mode (see Self-Esteem buffer) resulted in a breakthrough idea that changed everything for good.

Having said that, be clear that if the stress you encounter becomes over-whelming and the coping strategies are not as effective as you need them to be, then summon the strength to get professional counseling. It's effective, short-term, and relatively inexpensive.

Job Aid – Stress Control

Step 1. Triggering Event

Prevent, avoid, fix, or remove the stressor. Reinterpret the meaning of the event. Practice different responses. Take breaks from the stressor.

Step 2. Thought Response

Make an optimistic appraisal first. Keep proper perspective. Develop viable options. Ask, "What's the worst thing that could happen?" Select the best option.

Step 3. Emotional Response

Change thinking to change the feeling. Call support network. Talk it out. Laugh.

Step 4. Physical Response

Six deep breaths. Get up and move. Take a walk. Tense and release muscles, and relax using imagery.

Step 5. Behavioral Response

List actions, set priorities, and take action. Assert yourself. Take a viable option. Adapt, accept, and welcome change.

11

Goal Setting for Success

Setting and achieving goals to get what you want

Objectives

It's easy to understand how people with goals accomplish significantly more than people without goals. Makes sense. People with goals have direction. They have a target that gives them something to work towards. This motivates them to achieve.

If the goal is something you really want, that strong positive emotional desire gives you a favorable edge to realizing the goal.

And the more frequently you review the goal, the more you focus on it, and the more you will recognize the resources and opportunities you need to move toward achieving your goal.

Motivation to achieve comes from having a clear target, developing a strong emotional desire, creating a doable action plan, allocating the resources (especially time), and taking action.

Business goals that align with personal goals are more motivating than goals that are not in alignment, unrelated in any way, or are counter to personal goals. Goals that help cause you to stretch increase your motivation.

Written goals provide a mechanism to review, refresh, and stay focused on what you want. People with written goals accomplish significantly more than people who only have goals in their heads.

After reading this chapter and working through the recommended activities you will know how to:

- Develop positive goal statements with measurable action plans
- Identify the resources you need and the source of those resources to achieve your goals
- Energize your goals using three powerful methods
- Select from multiple areas to set goals to create balance in your life

Definitions

There are many acceptable formats for goal statements, action plans, measurements, etc. What we'll focus on in this chapter is a definition that is consistently successful in clarifying and organizing goals in *many areas of a person's life – Positive Goals.*

A "positive goal" focuses on *what you want rather than what you don't want.* For example, "increase wins" rather than "decrease losses." You attract the object of your focus. If your focus is on "wins," then that's what you will get. If your focus is on "losses," then that's what you will get.

Goals that work consist of:

1. Positive Objective

- Positive Action Verb
- Positive Object (of the action)
- Clarifying Information

2. Measurable Target (Goal)

- Quantifiable

· Time-Limited

3. Deployment Strategy

  · Action Plan
  · Resources

4. Energizing Process

  · Imagery
  · Emotion
  · Affirmations

Goal Setting Format

To help you imagine what the result will look like, I've included the critical topics for the goal-setting format below.

Goal

Positive Objectives – Target – Timeline

Strategy

Action Plan to include a list of "action items," their "due date," and an indication of how you know its complete ("measure")

Resource / Source

List any "out of the ordinary" resources you might need that are not readily available, and identify the "sources" where you will get each of the resources you need. Time is a critical resource often overlooked or underestimated, resulting in many goals not being accomplished.

Energize Your Goal

  · Imagery (What does it look like? Photo available?)
  · Motivation (Why do it? Compelling event? Emotions attached to the goal?)

- Affirmations (Inspire you to continue toward achieving the goal

Goal Setting Process

Step 1: Positive Objective

An "Objective" is a statement that provides orientation and direction. An objective is the orienting component of a goal. Positive Objectives to be used in goal setting contain three components:

- a "positive" action verb
- a "positive" object
- clarifying information

Examples of Action Verbs

achieve, adapt, arrange, assemble, create, build, create, coordinate, collect, design, describe, develop, establish, evaluate, improve, initiate, install, inspire, maintain, make, manage, perform, plan, promote, participate, produce, prepare, recommend, satisfy, simplify, schedule, triple, transmit, unite, verify, write.

Examples of Clarified Objectives

Action: *Increase*

Object: *safety record*

Clarifying Information: *in all facilities, we own*

Action: *Contact*

Object: *current customers*

Clarifying Information: *regardless of size or location*

Action: *Participate in*

Object: *negotiations*

Clarifying Information: *with all major customers*

Action: *Answer*

Object: *phone*

Clarifying Information: *before the 4th ring*

Remember to use "positive" action verbs and objects rather than negative ones. For example, use "increase safety" rather than "decrease accidents." Or "increase responsiveness" rather than "reduce response time."

Step 2: Measurable Target is the GOAL

A goal is the measurable target of the objective, including a specified due date for the measurement(s) to take place.

The well-written goal statement has three components:

- **Positive Objective** - action-oriented with a clarified topic
- **Measurable target** - the goal itself
- **Time-Limit** - when it will be achieved

Example Goal Statements:
Clarified Objective: *Increase the number of contacts with previous customers to*
Measurable Target (Goal): *10 per week*
Time-Limit: *by January 20xx*
Clarified Objective: *Contact current customers*
Measurable Target (Goal): *to include all 300 named in the database*
Time-Limit: *by the end of the 3rd quarter*

Note that the wording can be reversed or mixed up as grammar and imagery dictate. This is acceptable as long as all the elements are present.

Step 3: Deployment Strategy

The deployment strategy has two components:

- Action plan: identifies the tasks to be done to achieve the goal

- Resources: determines what you need and where you'll get it (source) to complete the action items

Strategy: A game plan that identifies and lists the action items or key steps necessary to achieve the goal. Includes "what" to do, "when" to do it, and a measurement of how you know it's done.

Example Goal Statement and Action Plan

Goal Statement
(Objective, Measurable Target, Time limit)
Increase the number of closed service tickets by 10 per week by March 20xx.

Action Plan
(Note: Action items can be stated as topic areas or as complete objectives or goals)

Action Item: *Review the list of service tickets that take the longest to resolve to uncover what they have in common.*

- When? *Jan. 5, 20xx*
- Measure: *List of characteristics*

Action Item: *Analyze the reason for the delays in resolving the issues.*

- When? *Jan. 6, 20xx*
- Measure: *List of reasons*

Action Item: *Develop a plan to expedite the resolution of these problems that cause delays and meet with the manager to discuss and select cost-effective options.*

- When? *Feb. 1, 20xx*
- Measure: *Plan with optional ideas for resolving problems that usually take*

longer than they should. Also, develop meeting Agenda.

Action Item: *Schedule a meeting with the manager.*

- When? *Feb. 5, 20xx*
- Measure: *Meeting scheduled*

Action Item: *Attend a meeting.*

- When? *Feb. 7, 20xx*
- Measure: *Options selected. Feedback process defined. The action plan approved by a manager*

Action Item: Track progress results

- When? *Weekly*
- Measure: *Tracking form to be completed each week*

Action Item: *Develop compelling reasons and positive affirmations to motivate my success.*

- When? *Daily*
- Measure: *List of reasons to succeed. List of positive "self-talk" statements of affirmation*

Resources

The next component of the deployment strategy is to account for any resources you'll need and the source of those resources. Sometimes, you'll want to consider both Primary and Secondary resources and sources. If the primary resource (or source of that resource) is not available, you'll have to find an alternative or secondary resource (source).

An example would be when you're traveling down the primary road you take to work each day and find it blocked. You don't turn around and go home; you find an alternative route to take. You have a goal (get to work on time), so you may need to find a secondary resource if the primary one is not available.

One of the most important resources you can get is time! Often, we have everything except the time to pull it all together. Be sure you always allocate adequate time to complete each of the steps in the action plan.

One question and concern that sometimes comes up from time to time relates to having the necessary resources to achieve the goal. Just keep this in mind: once you clearly define your goal, at some point in time, so long as you keep looking, the resources you need will find their way to you! How is that possible? Because until you know what it looks like, you won't see it, even if it's sitting right in front of you right now! But be aware the resource might not be in the form you initially thought it would take.

For example, you might think you need a certain amount of money to buy a computer, and then someone comes along and offers you the one they no longer use. Or you might think you need some amount of money to pay for something such as tuition but don't have a job. And then along comes someone who needs things done and is willing to pay you to do it, and instantly you've created your own job earning the money you need. Always be on the lookout for ways to meet your functional needs.

Examples of some resources and sources you may need including for a wide range of goals:

Resource - People:
 People with project knowledge
 Mentor with previous experience
 Time: 200 hours
 Source could be:
Human Resources budget to hire people with identified skills, hire a supervisor, and/or transfer current assignments to other staff in the department

Resource: Organizational structure:

Prescribed method of work

Sequence and time of resource utilization

Email list

Bound project report

Source could be:

Project management standards guide book

Special Work Flow Charts (PERT / GANT)

Project manager distribution list

Local copy company

Resource - Workspace:

Facilities of what nature and size (a place to work on your goal)

Equipment of what type and quantity

Materials of what type and quantity

Source could be:

Office space on the first floor in building B

Office equipment (included in office space)

Flip charts, markers, etc.

Resource - Other support:

Support from other departments

Resource directories, mailing lists

Source could be:

Project management

Company Library

TIPS:

1. Take inventory of where you are now. What resources do you currently have available to you that are needed to achieve your goal?
2. If other people are going to be affected, get them involved. Tell them what you plan to do and ask for their help and support.

3. Be aware of what you will "not" be doing or getting while carrying out your action plan.

Step 4: Energizing Your Goals

The next step is to generate the level of motivation you need to handle challenges related to achieving the goal. Persistence pays. The process of providing motivation contains three components that "energize the goal:"
You energize your goal by using appropriate:

- Imagery
- Emotion
- Affirmations

Imagery is more than "visualization." You can imagine the smell of fresh-baked bread or the taste of bittersweet lemon, or what it feels like to touch cold steel, or what a favorite song sounds like as you listen to it in your mind.
Involve the five physical senses to imagine what it will be like when you achieve this goal.

Imagine the "end result."

- *What will that look like?*
- *What will that smell like?*
- *What will that taste like?*
- *What will that feel (touch) like?*
- *What will that sound like?*

See yourself in possession of the goal. Just imagine you can see, smell, taste, touch, and hear it! Get pictures of it or pictures of what it represents to you. Engage the full range of emotion that accompanies the physical and sensory experience.
Recall similar memories of something that you've experienced in the past.

Generate the full sensory image, including emotions, of this previous success and, in your mind, replace the previous goal with the one you are now seeking.

If the goal is tangible, like a new car, go to the dealership and test drive it. Spend time in it, absorbing the whole sensory experience.

Get photos, samples, perhaps something related that represents the goal, and anything else that makes it more real to you. Look at them daily and re-create the whole sensory experience when you do.

Emotion motivates. Answer the questions: *"Why do it?"* *"What is the 'compelling event?"* *"Why now?"* Use the "Create Attitudes Instantly" skills.

For stretch goals requiring a degree of effort, you will need both your conscious and subconscious minds working together to achieve them. It's not uncommon for the conscious mind to want something and the subconscious mind to be programmed to accomplish something different. When this happens, the goal can be unwittingly sabotaged by old mental conditioning that hasn't been replaced with new thought patterns to support the goal.

Thoughts energized by emotions in a physically and mentally relaxed state directly influence previously programmed habits being carried out by the subconscious mind.

One way you can do this is by daydreaming. Find a place where you won't be disturbed for 2 to 5 minutes, relax and daydream about achieving your goal. Use full sensory imagery. Repeat this exercise for 66 consecutive days. Just "imagine" what it is like to have what you want!

Another way is to read your goal statement just before you sleep at night and let yourself experience the full sensory imagery plus the emotions of joy that will come when you achieve your goal. Keep the end result of the goal in front of you as often as possible. Review your list of goals first thing in the morning. Keep photos or other representations of your goals where you can see them.

The **"Law of Dominant Thought"** says that whatever you keep in the forefront of your mind constantly and consistently is what you will begin to move toward unconsciously. Action follows thought.

When your mind enthusiastically (emotionally) wraps around an idea, it creates the circumstances for it to be realized. You must, however, recognize the opportunity and take action.

"Create Supportive Attitudes" is a process that enables you to strengthen a belief and turn it into an attitude! How? Take any belief or behavior and challenge it with the question "why?" Be sure to use a challenging tone. With others you must be gentle and make sure they successfully defend their goals. Do the same with yourself.

When you challenge, you automatically elicit the defense emotions. The more you defend an idea, belief, or behavior, the more entrenched it becomes and the more resistant to change it becomes. This is how you create attitudes. Challenge yourself with the question, "WHY?"

"Why do I want to achieve this goal?" Now, challenge the response, then challenge that response and continue to challenge each answer until you get to the core value.

Continue these repeated challenges, always making sure you win (or the person you're challenging wins).

- *"Why is this goal important to me?"*
- *"What will I get out of it?"*
- *"What will happen if I don't achieve it?"*
- *"Why don't I want that?"*

Imagery of the end result plus directly linked emotions (positive or negative) will motivate a prolonged effort.

The **"Law of Attraction"** states that "like attracts like," so what you continually think about, imagine, and experience with emotion creates a vibration frequency that continues to grow with time. That vibration then resonates with similar things vibrating at a similar frequency, and the two eventually will come together after consistent emotionally charged, clearly imagined outcomes. One will cause the manifestation of the other. This is much like tuning forks that, once struck, will cause other tuning forks of the same note to vibrate, but not the others.

Goal Statements that rhyme: A little-known fact rarely brought out when discussing goals is that goal statements that rhyme engages the brain's right hemisphere more so than those that don't. Goal statements with emotion with music help carry the goal from the logical, literal left brain across the corpus callosum to the right brain. Chants, songs, music, and rhymes can also elicit emotions, providing a whole-brain approach, especially when adding full sensory imagery and emotion.

Using affirmations appropriately will help. We all talk to ourselves. You probably just said in your mind something like, "that's right," or, "I wonder if I do that?" Listen carefully to things you tell yourself that counter achieving your goal. For example, "I could never do that." There are many resources available where you can find inspirational statements to say to yourself that support your goals. Positive "affirmations" are essential to re-programming some of the old self-defeating tapes that play over and over in our heads.

Positive affirmations that have a significant impact follow these simple rules:

1. **Present Tense:** They are stated in the present tense. "I am" rather than "I will become." "I am in the process of becoming..." is an acceptable alternative when you just know you're not yet there.
2. **Specific:** Engage full sensory imagination in as much detail as you can. Keep practicing and adding more and more detail to the imagery of the result.
3. **Conviction:** Add more and different emotions by saying your statements with positive determination, conviction, and commitment. Then feel the joy of accomplishment supplied by the imagery.
4. **Repetition, repetition, repetition:** Every day, without fail, read one or

more of your positive affirmations that keeps you inspired and on track. High levels of consistent repetition are needed to form a habit. Recent research by Phillippa Lally and others and published in the *European Journal of Social Psychology* (2009), says that it takes an average of 66 days to form a habit but could take a lot less (18 days) for simple habits and much longer (256 days) for more complex habits working against competing habits.

5. **Ask,** "What is the one thing I can do today that will take me closer to achieving my goal?" Record it and do it. Then, "How can I make this into a goal-sustaining habit?"

Examples of Positive Affirmations:

- *I pay the price for achieving that which I desire.*
- *Never risking failure means never getting the chance to succeed.*
- *I do the most productive thing possible every moment of the day.*
- *My beliefs are my destiny; my desire is my power.*
- *With each step of action I take, I come closer to achieving my goal.*
- *Is what I'm doing, thinking, and feeling moving me closer to my goal?*
- *Once I've set my goal, I give no thought to failure. I expect to win!*
- *I succeed beyond my wildest expectations because I dare to have high expectations.*
- *I can achieve great and small things because I know what great and small things I want to achieve.*
- *If I can imagine it with accurate detail, I can achieve it, or I wouldn't have been able to imagine it in the first place.*

Areas of Life to Set Goals

Set goals in many areas of your life to maintain balance. There are many ways to organize the different areas of your life that are important to you and important to others in your life.

1. **Personal** (mental, physical, spiritual)

2. **Family** (immediate, relatives)
3. **Social** (friendships, networks)
4. **Professional** (education, career path)
5. **Financial** (income, wealth management, retirement)
6. **Possessions** (car, boat, house, computer, bicycle, clothes)
7. **Lifestyle** (modern, conservative, country, urban, suburban, sophisticated, stylish

Attempt to **align your goals** to become **mutually supportive** rather than conflict with each other. For example, modifying your lifestyle could lead to one that enables greater outdoor activities and helps to achieve a personal physical fitness goal. Whereas spending all your available time pursuing one goal leaves little energy left for anything else that's important to you.

Writing goals helps you focus on what you want. It enables the subconscious mind to find opportunities for you to get what you want. Look at each of the different areas of your life and see what you've got. That will tell you what you're focusing on and what you're not focusing on. To attain the most extraordinary levels of achievement, create mutually supportive goals.

One of the self-talk affirmations, *"I do the most productive thing possible every moment of the day,"* can begin to cause problems if we only focus on setting goals in one area of our life. For example, if you only set goals for your work life, you will become very accomplished. But what will you give up for that? What about family, personal growth, social, and physical goals to achieve balance?

Consider gaining balance in your life. You do this by setting goals in each of the different areas of your life. Set one short-range goal, one mid-range goal, and one long-range goal for each area of your life that is important to you! Remember, you begin to achieve your long-range goals by the actions you take today. For example, you've heard people in their later years say that they wish they had started investing for their future earlier in life, even if it were just a couple of dollars a month. By taking action now, you'll succeed in achieving your goal that may be set for 30 years from now. Once you accomplish a goal in any area, replace it with another.

Some examples of *objectives* that could be turned into goals by adding the measurable target (goal), action plan, and resources. For now, they stand as examples to represent the different areas of a person's life to show balance.

Personal: Physical Area:

Short-range: Design a healthy nutrition plan. Eat healthily.

Mid-range: Select hobbies that will keep me active and engaged.

Long-range: Exercise to maintain health.

Family Area:

Short-range: Have a special event of any duration every week.

Mid-range: Live, teach, and instill select values in children.

Long-range: Maintain a close positive relationship of love and trust.

Social: Friends Area:

Short-range: Develop friendships with people I like.

Mid-range: Find and meet people with shared interests and strong chemistry to build close relationships.

Long-range: Keep in touch with close friends.

Professional Area:

Short-range: Finish bachelor's degree by next fall.

Mid-range: Obtain recognition from a professional association.

Long-range: Conduct research and publish findings.

Financial Area:

Short-range: Create a prosperous mentality and money-matter positive habits.

Mid-range: Spend wisely to live below our means and achieve our financial planning goals.

Long-range: Plan, invest, and save for long-term financial security.

Possessions: Home Area:

Short-range: Rent an apartment located close to work to save commute time and money.

Mid-range: Lease a home located close to work in a stable neighborhood.

Long-range: Buy a home, condo, or town home that will meet our family's needs.

Lifestyle Area:

Short-range: Identify the characteristics of an active, social, urban, and healthy lifestyle to emulate.

Mid-range: Maintain physical conditioning and weight, size, and shape goals.

Long-range: Seek a retirement community that will provide for our chosen lifestyle.

Create your own objectives from your own dreams, and challenge them relentlessly to ensure you've worked on those that matter most and now have strong attitudes to support them.

Achieving Goals Step by Step Summary

So now you can see that balancing life takes setting goals in more than one area. The great thing about setting multiple goals is that with some planning, you can leverage one off another and accomplish them in less time with less effort.

There is no doubt in my mind that you are now equipped to begin the process of setting and achieving goals. Don't wait to get started. Do it now. Take a sheet of paper and start listing the areas and what you'd like to accomplish on a short, mid, and long-term basis. This will take a few days to flush out thoroughly, so keep the paper out and visible so that it can be added to at any time the inspiration hits you.

Review the goals you have so far, set priorities, and write the action items on your calendar and the pictures on the wall showing the results of your goal and what it means to you and those affected by it. Once you have set a reasonable course, stay focused, and **give no thought to failure**. Stay away from the "naysayers" (don't share these goals with people who might shoot them down in the name of not wanting you to get your hopes up). And finally, be happy that you know how to get what you want step-by-step!

About the Author

Robert "Bob" DeGroot MEd, DCH, is the founder of Sales Training International and the SalesHelp brand owner. He is a bestselling author, psychometric researcher, test developer, consultant, top-producing sales professional, and trainer.

After completing his military service in the US Coast Guard, Bob attended Texas State University, earning a Bachelor of Arts degree in Psychology and a Master of Education (MEd) in School Psychology. He earned his Doctor of Clinical Hypnotherapy (DCH) degree from the American Institute of Hypnotherapy.

He is the author of *Psychology for Successful Selling* (Branden Publishing Company, 1988). The book that launched his company. Since then, Bob has written over 70 training courses and 50 Web-based training courses and published dozens of bestselling eBooks in the professions of sales, sales management, and customer service. See www.SalesHelp.com.

You can connect with me on:

🌐 https://www.saleshelp.com

Also by Robert DeGroot

Sales Titles

Value Selling Strategies P.R.O.S.P.E.C.T. Model (Best Seller)

Strategic Sales Plan (Best Seller)

Objection Free Selling (Best Seller)

Features, Advantages, Benefits (Best Seller)

Negotiating Value (Best Seller)

Benefit Questions Create Attitudes (Best Seller)

Block the Competition

Trust & Rapport Building (also Customer Service Title)

Goal Setting for Success (Best Seller – also Customer Service Title)

Competitor Analysis

Closing Strategies of the Masters (Best Seller)

Sales Prospecting: The Hunt for New Business (includes the following short eBooks)

Profile and Qualify (Best Seller)

Key Decision Maker Roles (Best Seller)

Research Prospect & Competitor

Telephone Cold Call and Voicemail Strategies (Best Seller)

Email Prospecting (includes two bestsellers)

Networking Contact Strategy (Best Seller)

Asking for Referrals

Teleblitz (Best Seller)

Funnel Management (Best Seller)

Ratio Management (Best Seller)

Time & Territory Management

Sales Management Titles

Reseller Strategy (Best Seller)

Career Path for Sales Professionals

Interviewing and Hiring

Sales Professionals Performance Appraisal

Sales Coach

Peer-to-Peer Sales Coaching (Best Seller)

Creating and Leading a Motivating Sales Culture

Effective Meeting Planning and Facilitating

Customer Service Titles – Available individually for purchase

Create Attitudes Instantly

Telephone Etiquette for Business (Best Seller)

Email Etiquette for Business (Best Seller)

Trust and Rapport Building (also Sales Title)

Active Listening Skills for Business (Best Seller)

Problem-Solving Model for Business (Best Seller)

Defusing Customer Anger (Best Seller)

Managing Customer Expectations (Best Seller)

Creating Customer Loyalty

Stress Control at Work

Goal Setting for Success (Best Seller – also Sales Title)